An Interactive Journey to
Spiritual Growth

MICHAELA L. CARSON

WESTBOW
PRESS®
A DIVISION OF THOMAS NELSON
& ZONDERVAN

Copyright © 2022 Michaela L. Carson.

All rights reserved. No part of this book may be used or reproduced by any means, graphic, electronic, or mechanical, including photocopying, recording, taping or by any information storage retrieval system without the written permission of the author except in the case of brief quotations embodied in critical articles and reviews.

This book is a work of non-fiction. Unless otherwise noted, the author and the publisher make no explicit guarantees as to the accuracy of the information contained in this book and in some cases, names of people and places have been altered to protect their privacy.

WestBow Press books may be ordered through booksellers or by contacting:

WestBow Press
A Division of Thomas Nelson & Zondervan
1663 Liberty Drive
Bloomington, IN 47403
www.westbowpress.com
844-714-3454

Because of the dynamic nature of the Internet, any web addresses or links contained in this book may have changed since publication and may no longer be valid. The views expressed in this work are solely those of the author and do not necessarily reflect the views of the publisher, and the publisher hereby disclaims any responsibility for them.

Any people depicted in stock imagery provided by Getty Images are models, and such images are being used for illustrative purposes only.
Certain stock imagery © Getty Images.

Author photo: Wild Sun Photography

Unless otherwise indicated, all Scripture quotations are taken from the Holy Bible, New Living Translation, copyright © 1996, 2004, 2015 by Tyndale House Foundation. Used by permission of Tyndale House Publishers, Carol Stream, Illinois 60188. All rights reserved.

Scripture quotations taken from The Holy Bible, New International Version® NIV®
Copyright © 1973 1978 1984 2011 by Biblica, Inc. TM
Used by permission. All rights reserved worldwide.

ISBN: 978-1-6642-6846-3 (sc)
ISBN: 978-1-6642-6847-0 (hc)
ISBN: 978-1-6642-6845-6 (e)

Library of Congress Control Number: 2022910672

Print information available on the last page.

WestBow Press rev. date: 08/09/2022

# Contents

Dedication .................................................................... vii
Foreword ....................................................................... ix
A Note from Michaela ................................................. xi
Embarking on Your Interactive Faith Journey ............ xiii

## Part 1: Discipline

Heart Soil ...................................................................... 1
Perfect Father ............................................................... 6
Disciplined Disciples .................................................. 10
Safe Sanctuary ............................................................ 14
Resolute Resolutions .................................................. 20

## Part 2: Prayer

The Taproot ................................................................ 29
Gratitude ..................................................................... 34
Repentance ................................................................. 40
Requests ..................................................................... 46
Listen .......................................................................... 52
Persistence ................................................................. 58

## Part 3: Scripture

The Root System ........................................................ 67
Healthy Digestion ....................................................... 72
Hear Him Speak ......................................................... 76
Learn Truth ................................................................. 82
Apply and Grow .......................................................... 86
Memorize and Fight ................................................... 90

## Part 4: Community

The Forest .......................................................................... 99
Worship ............................................................................ 104
Fellowship ........................................................................ 110
Restored Relationships ..................................................... 116
Unity ................................................................................. 122
Discipleship ...................................................................... 126

Acknowledgements ........................................................... 131
Author Bio ........................................................................ 133

# Dedication

This book is dedicated to my mom, who began my faith journey; my husband, who has traveled the road alongside me for nearly thirty years; my daughter, who taught me deeper levels of trust in the Lord than I could have ever imagined; and to every person who has walked a minute or a mile on this path with me. Thank you.

# Foreword

The team sat around the table reviewing the just completed curriculum we had written for our small group ministry. As a groups pastor in ministry for more than twenty years, I was excited for our people to experience this next step in discipleship. Our congregation covers many faith backgrounds—from staunch Catholic to swinging-from-the-chandeliers Pentecostal to those who have never before set foot in a church. I knew the original Bible study materials would enable us to provide content that met people where they were in the faith while helping them grow closer to Jesus. Michaela surprised me that day, though, as I have seen her do before. She began asking some difficult questions about connecting with new believers who had never read their Bibles before while continuing to minister to the mature group participants. She also asked about some of the middle steps we had overlooked in the discipleship process and expressed her concerns about embracing any church discipleship trends that seemed flashy but would not actually anchor our people in God's Word. These questions challenged me. I realized I had been in the church world for too long and had become disconnected from the new believer's perspective. How could I walk our people through discipleship if I wasn't connecting with them on every step of their faith journey?

Jesus said in the Great Commission to go into all the world and make disciples—not converts. Michaela Carson has a passion for doing precisely that. She pulls from years of experience pastoring alongside her husband and combines that with perspectives from group members in various studies she has led. She has the unique ability to see discipleship and relationship with Jesus through the eyes of both one who has never cracked open a Bible and one who has taught the Bible. I have seen her walk individuals through how to study Scripture, even when understanding it felt daunting to them. I have seen her teach people how to pray personally and in front of others and how to get the most out of journaling. You will find she is not afraid of the hard questions. She does not shy away from accountability or confrontation. She has personally modeled a life of surrender and obedience, which led to growth in discipleship. Every pastor, as well as every follower of Christ, would benefit from her insights on making disciples. She can help you ask questions you never thought to ask, whether for yourself or your congregation!

So prepare to be challenged. Prepare to grow. Just like I did in our curriculum meeting that day, prepare to question your approach to discipleship. Prepare to go deeper!

Angi Jeffcoat
Connections Pastor, Ocean Church

# A Note from Michaela

To the ones whose hearts want more,

I was so young that I don't remember when I gave my heart to Jesus—the moment He saved me. I do know that it was before I was five—before my dad died. I know because I ran to Him when I missed my earthly father. Salvation is only the beginning of walking with Him. We must also reach a point of surrender...when He isn't just our Savior, He is our Lord. That exact moment I do know: January 13, 1990. I was at a retreat with my youth group when He asked me to let go of everything that mattered to me and choose Him. So I did. I remember the moment He told me that I would marry a pastor. And I did. I remember a lot of things along my faith journey, and not all of them are good. I remember when, as a pastor's wife, I struggled even to want to spend time with God in prayer or reading the Bible. I remember when worship felt like songs to sing and not the outpouring of my heart. I remember telling people that I would pray for them, then promptly forgetting to do so. And I remember the struggle of not wanting just to look the part and say the right things, but to walk in the disciplines I knew everyone else had, but I didn't. I remember feeling lost and having no clue how to change things. I wish that realization had been my turning point, but it wasn't. It was another five years before I understood that something had to change. Getting by wasn't enough anymore, and I was tired of being stuck. I needed to go deeper in my relationship with God, but how?

If you feel stuck, like I was, I pray that sharing what the Holy Spirit has taught me will help you find the strength to try something new—again. If you are totally on fire for Jesus but lack the discipline to serve Him in joyful obedience, I pray the strategies in these pages teach you a fresh way to love Him. If you have walked with Him and followed Him for years but have never kept a faith journal, I hope you will learn how easy and important it is to chronicle your story of faith.

No matter where you are in your relationship with God, there is one thing that we all need—to go deeper.

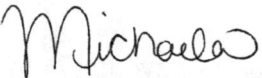

# Embarking on Your Interactive Faith Journey

Designed to be customized for you, this book meets you right where you are. Use what works and forget what doesn't. When you're stuck, try something new because the same old thing clearly isn't working. We know that the definition of insanity is doing the same thing over and over again and expecting different results, yet this is something we do regularly in our faith lives. Why? Because we build an idea of what we think our faith lives should look like and keep trying to force it into that mold. For example, daily time with God means that I get up at 5 a.m., make a fresh pot of coffee, sit on my lanai watching a beautiful sunrise, and then spend deep and meaningful time with the Lord. When we think that is what our daily time with Him should look like, we are disappointed ten out of ten times. That constant dissatisfied leads to discouragement, and discouragement leads to giving up. So what if we stop expecting perfection? What if we accept where we are and who we are? Could we maybe go deeper with God if we set aside our expectations and started seeking His?

**Step 1—Accept that perfect isn't perfect.** It's ideal. Perfect is daily walking with Jesus. If you are doing that, then you are meeting His expectations. Anything more is your own expectation.

**Step 2—Accept that you are you** and not your best friend, the pastor's wife, or your spiritual mentor. God meets you where *you* are, not where they are. So stop comparing and seek His plan for *you*.

**Step 3—Let go of your expectations.** Literally. Confess them to God and say, "This is no longer what I want; I just want you, Lord."

**Step 4—Try again.** Try something new. Stretch your comfort level and do what He's been asking you to do. Do the thing that sounds too easy (or too hard), too confusing (or too simple), too wild (or too dull). Just try it. Keep reading this book, for example.

I wrote this book to help you figure it out. Each chapter focuses on one aspect of how we can go deeper in our relationships with God, and that is not the same for me as it is for you. Listen for the Holy Spirit to prompt you. If something catches your attention or stands out to you, highlight it or make a note. You will find three separate sections at the end of each chapter with three different opportunities to explore. I call this "Map Your Journey" because our faith walks are exactly that—an interactive journey that we create with the Lord. Since none of us are the same, we all have different needs.

The goal isn't to do all of the prompts every day. The idea is to find the one that God is asking you to explore. Let His Spirit lead you. You may find in some chapters that you need to sit on the concept for a little while, so explore more of the prompts. There may be moments of "Yes, I've got this!" There is no right or wrong. If it takes you a day, a week, or a month to complete a chapter, then that is precisely the time it was meant to take. It is your story that you and God are writing, and it shouldn't look like mine or your mom's or that lady in your small group's. It is yours—uniquely and perfectly yours. I invite you to write the next chapter of your faith story, just you and Jesus.

All you need to take the next step is a journal and a willingness to be led by the Spirit as you create your interactive faith journey.

## *What is a Faith Journal?*

I have kept many different types of journals over the years—prayer journals, sermon notes, reflective thoughts, Bible studies, writing prompts and ideas, etc. The trouble was that they each told a part of my story; not one of them told the entire story. So in 2019, I tried something new. I bought a new journal and made it my faith journal—a journal designed to tell my complete story. I use the same journal for everything I once kept in separate journals. Having a chronological and comprehensive record gives me a clearer picture of how and when God works in my life. Now when I look back, I see the sermon that prompted the reflection and then the prayer of repentance that came out of it—all in one place.

Whether you're a "writer" or not, I highly recommend that you try keeping a faith journal while reading this book. This has been one of the most pivotal turning points for me personally. Often in Scripture (approximately four hundred times!), we read about someone building an altar to the Lord. Why? Altars were memorials of the places where God met them; they were places of encounter, forgiveness, worship, covenant, and intercession. We don't have an opportunity in our society to physically construct reminders of our encounters with God, but we do have journaling. It is an effective way to memorialize when God "alters" us. So, whether you think it's for you or not, can I challenge you to try it? Maybe, just maybe, writing out these moments will be part of your journey deeper. For those ready to take that step, here are some tips to get started:

1. **Pick a journal**—maybe it's a spiral notebook, a file on your computer or an app on your phone. It needs to be something you're comfortable with, and it doesn't matter in the least how it looks.
2. **Decide to use it**—we always have a choice. Go all in, at least for the duration of this book. If you finish and

still think journaling isn't for you, that's okay; at least you tried.
3. **Use it daily**—even if you aren't reading this book every day, begin to develop the discipline of daily recording God's work in your life.
4. **Use YOUR voice**—not everyone is a writer, but you can write if you can read (which I know you can). If the idea of composing paragraphs intimidates you, don't write in paragraphs—try bullet points, single sentence responses, or even keywords that mean something to you.

Remember, there is no right or wrong way to build your altar, and the tools are up to you!

## *How to Map Your Journey*

For this to be an interactive book, you get to do some of the heavy lifting! At the end of each chapter, you will find a "Map Your Journey" page made up of three sections. It is important to remember that our time with the Lord isn't another item to check off our to-do lists. Depending on your personality, you may be tempted to complete every item on the "list." Don't! It's not a list. Resist the compulsion. Read through all the options and select one or two that stand out to you each day. If a chapter hits a nerve and the topic is something that God wants you to ponder a little longer, then do one or two prompts the first day. The next day, reread the chapter and do another one or two prompts. It's okay to spend a week and complete all of the prompts. Just don't do it because you think you "have to," and don't rush to finish it because that ultimately defeats the purpose.

**Journal Prompts**—These are reflective questions about where you are in your faith and what God is doing in you right now. Answer any that speak to you in your faith journal. Remember, the purpose of journaling is to help us live out Psalm 77:11: "But then I recall all you have done, O LORD; I remember your wonderful deeds of long ago." It helps us remember the things the enemy wants us to forget.

**Deeper Study**—These chapter topics offer additional Scripture verses to delve into when there is an idea you want to explore further. If a verse speaks to you, write it out in your faith journal and include any thoughts about what God is saying to you. The more we read and understand His Word, the better we can share it with others. Sometimes this takes effort, but Paul teaches us in 2 Timothy 2:15 that it's important: "Work hard so you can present yourself to God and receive his approval. Be a good worker, one who does not need to be ashamed and who correctly explains the word of truth."

**Our Model**—Jesus is our perfect example. Always. This section provides Scripture references that connect to the chapter topics and help us look closely at the life and teachings of Jesus to better model our faith after Him. Ephesians 5:1–2 tells us to "Imitate God, therefore, in everything you do, because you are his dear children. Live a life filled with love, following the example of Christ. He loved us and offered himself as a sacrifice for us, a pleasing aroma to God."

I am so glad that you have decided to take this adventure. I hope that sharing my struggle to go deeper with the Lord will help you. As I share what He has taught me, I pray that the Holy Spirit speaks to you as well. But I also pray that He teaches you something different. Why? Because your faith journey is your story, not mine.

# Part 1
## Discipline

*"We are called to put down deep roots in a shallow world."*
—Josh Hall

# Heart Soil

*Then Christ will make his home in your hearts as you trust in him.*
*Your roots will grow down into God's love and keep you strong.*
—EPHESIANS 3:17

The only way that we can grow in any relationship is to spend time with that person. It's easy to know what that looks like in our human relationships, but what about intimacy with our Creator? That doesn't seem as straightforward. We start by examining the condition of our own hearts.

The soil in the Parable of the Sower found in Matthew 13 is reflective of our hearts. When God's Word is spoken to a hardened heart, it is like a seed that falls on the path. Since it's not received, there is no root. Because there is no root, the birds come and snatch the seed. Since you are reading this book, that is not you, even if you think it is. If you truly hardened your heart against God, you wouldn't be seeking a way to deepen your relationship with Him.

The next example Jesus gives us is of the seeds that *do* take root. Interestingly, the first root that grows from a seed is the taproot. The sole initial purpose of the taproot is to penetrate deep into the earth and find water. Throughout Scripture, water is often a symbol of God's Spirit—of His Presence. So, it makes sense that seeking His presence through prayer is the first thing we do when we enter our relationships with Christ. It is the very first root of our growth in Him. Many of us prayed even before we surrendered control of our lives to Christ, but there was no depth or genuine source of water until we realized we needed a Savior. That prayer is the one that changed everything. It's no longer about "personal growth" or "being a better person"; it's about our growth as Christ followers. God has created something new in us, and for the purpose of this book we will look at that new thing as a tree.

So our very first root sprouts from a prayer of desperation. We cry out to God, desperate for a Savior, desperate for forgiveness, desperate for freedom. This root is powerful! It plunges into the darkness of the earth, searching for the water that can bring forth life. And when it finds that Living Water—whoa! Relief and refreshment flood our hearts! Our seeds of faith have sprouted their first root, and it is good.

Sadly, many stop there, never realizing that faith is a journey, not a moment. According to Jesus, these are the seeds the farmer scatters that land on rocks; they initially grow quickly but never develop deep roots because their heart soils are shallow. With only one root, they can't take in enough water and nutrients to support the sprout; when the sun's heat beats down, they die.

Then there was the seed that fell on fertile soil—a heart ready for more of God. That seed? Watch out, world! That seed is destined to be a mighty oak tree. Strong. Solid. Unshakeable. So how do we go from a seed in shallow soil to a tree with deep roots? Well, it is the condition of our hearts. First, we must desire to grow. We must cultivate our hearts so that this can happen. It starts with longing. Our journey deeper begins with a fertile heart that is ready for growth.

*So our very first root sprouts from a prayer of desperation. We cry out to God, desperate for a Savior, desperate for forgiveness, desperate for freedom. This root is powerful!*

## Map Your Journey

As you build your first "altar," remember, the goal isn't to finish the list; it's to allow the Holy Spirit space to speak. Take a moment and pray. Ask the Lord to show you where He is providing you an opportunity to grow. When you finish, read through the three sections below. Select one or two bullet points to focus on and record your reflections in your faith journal.

### Journal Prompts

- With which of these soils (hardened, shallow, or fertile) does your heart connect today? What do you feel is your normal soil type? Are you happy with where you are?
- If you believe your roots are shallow right now, what might the Holy Spirit be leading you to do? How might you go deeper today?
- If you connect with the fertile soil and your heart is in a good place, how can you fertilize your desire for more of God? What can you do to make sure your soil stays healthy?

### Deeper Study

- **Roots**
  Jeremiah 17:7–8; Luke 6:48–49;
  Ephesians 3:17–18; Colossians 2:6–7
- **Heart Condition**
  Psalms 26:2, 51:10, 139:23–24; Matthew 6:21
- **Desiring God**
  Psalms 42:1, 63:8, 73:25; Jeremiah 29:13

## *Our Model*

We must look to Jesus as our example for spiritual health. Sometimes we learn from how He responded to situations, and at other times, we can look directly at His teachings about an issue. Take a few minutes to read through Matthew 6:19–24. When you're done, jot down your thoughts about this passage and its relation to the fertility of your own heart's soil.

# Perfect Father

*The LORD is like a father to his children, tender and compassionate to those who fear him.*

—PSALM 103:13

Life is hard. When we choose to follow Jesus, it doesn't get easier; it gets harder. The real difference for Christ followers is that we have a Source of strength Who makes the struggles of this life worth something. Most of the time, hard things feel hard because we can't control them. "If this would happen," or "if this hadn't happened," life would be so much easier. Well, those things are generally beyond our power. If my father hadn't died... If my wife hadn't left... If my son had just listened to me... If my boss appreciated how hard I worked... The list goes on. So how do we live the abundant life Jesus promises in John 10:10? He said, "The thief's purpose is to steal and kill and destroy. My purpose is to give them a rich and satisfying life." Clearly, there are two sides to the coin.

The formula isn't hard to understand, but it isn't what most of us want it to be either. Nearly all of us wish for a genie who does what we ask, but that isn't the God we learn about in the Bible. Paul explains it quite simply in Romans 6:16, "Don't you realize that you become the slave of whatever you choose to obey? You can be a slave to sin, which leads to death, or you can choose to obey God, which leads to righteous living." It all boils down to obedience. Not in a legalistic or ritualistic way but in the way a child obeys a loved and respected parent. We don't obey because we fear punishment; we obey out of a deep love for our Father.

Surrendering control in every aspect of our lives to a loving Father, seeking counsel from His Holy Spirit, and following the teaching of His beloved Son leads us into a deeper relationship with Him. It's overwhelming to consider that the God of the universe—the Creator of everything—wants an intimate relationship with us. Depending on our religious backgrounds, or lack of one, we tend to see God as either a firm authoritarian or a loving Father. In actuality, He is both. He is Sovereign (Acts 4:24); He is the Supreme Ruler who answers to no one. Yet He is also Abba Father (Romans 8:15). While the original word, άββα, has no equivalent in the English language, it is a term for "father" that is both a title of authority and an expression of warm affection and loving confidence.

As an American, submitting to a sovereign goes against everything we are taught. We like democracy—everyone gets an equal vote and has a right to be heard—but this is not God's plan for us spiritually. We generally love the idea of a permissive Father, one who gives us what we want. But God is a perfect Father. Because He is sovereign, He actually knows what is best for us at every moment and in every situation. We can always trust Him because, unlike our earthly fathers, He is all-knowing and does not make mistakes. Numbers 23:19 teaches us that God is not like us; He does not lie, and He does not change His mind. He has never spoken and failed to act or made a promise He did not keep. Every direction in which He leads us, everything He asks us to do, is for our good (Romans 8:28). He is not a dictator who controls people like puppets, and He is not a Father who gives us what we want so we'll like Him or stop pestering Him.

If we do not understand the true nature of our heavenly Father, our path becomes precarious. When we do not understand His heart, we risk every step of obedience we take becoming a march toward legalism. Every prayer of negotiation is another paver on a dangerous road we build in an attempt to manipulate God to our will.

## Map Your Journey

Today take some time to reflect on how you view God, and if there is anything in your understanding of Him that contradicts Scripture, take the time to work it out with Him in prayer by confessing any concepts you've been holding onto that minimize who He is. That is the first step in going deeper in your faith journey. Then, read through all of the prompts and select one or two to focus on today.

### Journal Prompts

- Do you view God more as an authoritarian dictator or a permissive father? Why is that?
- Why do you have a hard time releasing control of the things you can't control? What are you afraid God will or won't do?
- Do you genuinely believe that everything God does in your life is with your best interest in mind? Why or why not?

### Deeper Study

- **God's Sovereignty**
  Isaiah 45:7–9; Acts 4:24; Ephesians 1:4; Colossians 1:16–17
- **God's Character**
  Numbers 23:19; Psalm 86:5; Romans 8:28; Hebrews 6:18; 1 John 4:8
- **Fear/Reverence for God**
  1 Samuel 12:24; Psalm 128:1; Matthew 10:29–31; Hebrews 12:28

## *Our Model*

As we walk our faith journeys, it can be easy to fall into the habit of working hard to please God, but it is essential to remember that the condition of our hearts determines our fruit. Godly actions pour from a heart that walks with God; sinful actions flow from a legalistic heart. Jesus offered powerful teaching to the religious leaders of His time. These leaders were knowledgeable about God but didn't fully understand His character—His Father's-heart. Read Matthew 23:23–26. His warning to those leaders is a warning for us today. We must examine our motives for the good we do and confess our pride when it appears. Write out a prayer confessing any areas the Holy Spirit reveals that might be more about doing good (actions we control) than being good (a heart surrendered to Him).

# Disciplined Disciples

*No discipline is enjoyable while it is happening—it's painful! But afterward there will be a peaceful harvest of right living for those who are trained in this way.*

—Hebrews 12:11

Many of us think we know what these words mean—discipline and disciple—but do we? It can be surprising how much our own experiences and societal worldviews can alter our perspectives.

First, let's look at "disciple" because discipline doesn't mean as much without it. Simply put, a disciple is a follower or student of a teacher, leader, or philosopher. Follower? An adherent or devotee of a particular person, cause, or activity. Adherent? Someone who supports a specific party, person, or set of ideas. Support? We could keep unpacking this for days... But the bottom line is that when Jesus talks about our being His disciples, He means that we follow His teachings. If you haven't noticed by now, not all of them are easy!

For many people, the word "discipline" has very negative connotations. So we need to address what this word truly means because it is crucial in the context of spiritual growth. Discipline means different things to each of us. For some, it triggers thoughts of punishment or even abuse; for others, it might be athleticism or healthy eating. Think about what it means to you. Maybe your first response was, "I don't have that!" or you thought of self-denial such as banning sweets, caffeine, television, etc. Maybe your mind even went to a form of self-punishment—pushing harder at the gym, working those extra hours to climb the next ladder rung.

When we explore the ideas of spiritual discipline, it is essential to understand the meaning of the word. One definition found in Merriam-Webster defines discipline as "training that corrects, molds, or perfects the mental faculties or moral character" and defines self-discipline as "correction or regulation of oneself for the sake of improvement." So, the first part of spiritual discipline is about controlling yourself. That means choosing to do something whether you "feel like it" or not (e.g., reading your Bible). Or, in some cases, choosing not to do something you know you shouldn't (e.g., cheating on your spouse). Spiritual discipline is *not* about punishment, pleasing God by following legalistic rules, or proving to anyone (including yourself) that you are good enough. Instead, authentic spiritual discipline is about growth. In the end, we want to say that we are closer to Jesus and know our Father better. Discipline makes us better disciples.

At the heart of any discipline is obedience. Whether you are following a program, a coach, or your own goals, you have to choose each day—each moment, really—to be obedient. Obedience is a word, like discipline, that many of us don't like. But let's unpack that for a moment. What is it that causes people to resist the idea? Is it fear of not being in control or someone else being in authority? If this is you, be careful. It is all too easy to slip into rebellion on the little things. A couple of loose pebbles can start a landslide that ultimately pulls you away from your faith. Maybe the idea of being obedient appeals to you. Some people view the world and their place in it as either black or white. They prefer knowing exactly what is expected. If this is you, use caution. It is all too easy to slip from heartfelt obedience to legalism when you view the world through a list of rules to be followed.

## Map Your Journey

Today take a few moments to reflect on your perceptions of discipleship, discipline, and obedience. Then, take those thoughts to God in prayer and allow Him to speak to you about them. After you pray, read through the prompts, and select one or two for journaling.

### *Journal Prompts*

- What words or images come to mind when you think of "discipline"? When you hear "self-discipline" does it conjure different imagery?
- Is there anything about the word "obedience" that makes you cringe a little? Why?
- Do you tend to lean toward rebellion or legalism? Ask God to show you why, and prayerfully consider what adjustments you might be able to make to better ground yourself against these slippery slopes.

### *Deeper Study*

- **Discipleship**
  Matthew 28:19–20; John 12:26; 1 Corinthians 4:16–17
- **Discipline**
  Proverbs 12:1; Proverbs 25:28; 1 Corinthians 9:27; Revelation 3:19
- **Obedience**
  1 Samuel 15:22; James 4:17; 1 John 2:3–6; 1 John 5:3

## Our Model

No one likes to be corrected; it's hard to accept correction or criticism. But Jesus rebuked His disciples when they needed it, when they were walking a path that wasn't His. Read Luke 9:46–56. Notice how the disciples were pursuing privilege and exclusivity. Reflect on Jesus' response, and prayerfully ask Him to reveal and rebuke any areas of wrong thinking in your own heart.

# Safe Sanctuary

*"...Although I have scattered you in the countries of the world, I will be a sanctuary to you during your time in exile."*
—Ezekiel 11:16

Have you ever felt abandoned? Unloved? Unwanted? Have you ever thought it was your fault or believed you deserved it? I can't count the times I've been in that darkness. Many of us only learn one part of God's character growing up. Many churches or families focus on one aspect of who He is; that isn't wrong, but it's not a complete picture either. None of us can fully understand God's character, but we can continue to learn more about who He is every day. When challenges and difficulties come, we often have a small-view version of God, and that tiny lens we are using may not be enough to get us through.

**God is Love.** This is a true statement, and the world (and the Church!) loves to focus on how loving He is. And that is not wrong. He does love each one of us exactly where we are. We do not have to do anything to earn His love. We cannot do anything to make Him love us more than He already does. But our flawed views of love and our singular focus on this one aspect of His character do not show us the entire picture.

**God is Just.** He cannot and will not abide sin. Some religions lead us to believe that we aren't good enough through this singular teaching, that we must live our lives trying to earn His love and our places in heaven. Our sin separates us from Him, so we must spend every day working to be better. This is a human attempt to obtain spiritual approval. We can never be good enough for a perfect God, so we strive and hope.

This belief that He demands perfection we cannot attain, by itself, is not enough.

**God is Forgiving.** Forgiveness is where love and justice meet. Because He is just, He wants our repentance. Because He is love, He offers His forgiveness. He is both love and just. He is forgiving. So what does that look like in real life? When we make the wrong choice, there are consequences. Because He loves us, He forgives us, but He doesn't wave a magic wand to remove the consequences. Instead, He offers us a safe place, a sanctuary, during the painful parts of our lives. Because He is love, He disciplines us when we go astray. Remember, He is not a permissive parent; He is a perfect and loving Father.

The nation of Israel's biggest and most frequent sin was idolatry. For us, it may be a career, a person, a platform, or even our own plans and desires—anything we prioritize above God. In the time and culture of the Old Testament, this was often quite literally idols; people turned from placing their complete trust in God and started putting some of it in the religion of the nations around them. This constant back and forth became the norm in their faith story. Finally, in the book of Ezekiel, God raised up a man to be His voice to the people. The back and forth was about to end. God was going to allow them to experience the full consequences of their continual sin. He allowed them to be conquered and taken captive by the Babylonians. As Ezekiel tells the people about the devastation to come (which they disregard), we find this statement "I will be your sanctuary during your time in exile." Even though they abandoned God, God was not abandoning them. Even though they rejected God, God was not rejecting them.

God does not change, and the same is true for us today. He does not abandon or reject us. However, when we choose to sin, we also must acknowledge that we deserve the consequences. My choice means my fault. I can turn to my Father and confess my sin, and He is faithful and just to forgive me and cleanse me from all unrighteousness (1 John 1:9). Jesus paid the eternal penalty for my sin, and I will see Him face-to-face one day. But

## DISCIPLINE

in this life, sin hurts God, ourselves, and other people. We impact this world when we sin, and sometimes it is a hard road to walk. If you are in that season, please remember, "Though your sins are like scarlet, [He] will make them as white as snow." (Isaiah 1:18) You can be fully forgiven. If you are walking through a wilderness of your own making, He is a sanctuary for you until you can return home.

*Forgiveness is where
love and justice meet.
Because He is just,
He wants our repentance.
Because He is love,
He offers His forgiveness.
He is both love and just.
He is forgiving.*

## Map Your Journey

Christ didn't overturn the law; He fulfilled it. Struggling to confess our sins to God and repent is either a pride issue or an unwillingness to stop sinning. Yet without confession, there is no forgiveness. Before reading through the prompts below, take a few moments to reflect on any habitual sin in your own life.

### *Journal Prompts*

- Where did your picture of God come from? What parts are accurate? What parts may not be?
- Which of these three attributes (love, just, forgiving) do you struggle with the most? Why is that?
- What aspects of God's character do you need to learn more about?

### *Deeper Study*

- **God is love**
  Proverbs 8:17; Jeremiah 31:3; Romans 5:8, 8:37–39
- **God is just**
  Exodus 34:6–7; Psalm 94:12; Hebrews 12:5–6
- **God is forgiving**
  2 Chronicles 7:14; Psalm 103:8–13; Micah 7:18–19; 1 John 1:9

## *Our Model*

Our society embraces the idea of a loving God—and sending His Son as our atoning sacrifice is the most loving act imaginable—but in Luke 16:13–15 Jesus teaches us that God's love doesn't negate justice for sin. Are there areas in which you are attempting to serve two masters? Do you have idols you need to release? Do you struggle with confessing your sin? How does your appearance in public differ from what's truly in your heart? Journal a prayer of confession and repentance so you can walk in your singular purpose.

# Resolute Resolutions

*"This is what the LORD of Heaven's Armies says: All this may seem impossible to you now... Be strong and finish the task!"*
—ZECHARIAH 8:6 & 9

When a new year is just around the corner, it isn't uncommon to start thinking about what you want to accomplish in the months to come. But like so many people, you may find that come February you've not been as successful as you had initially pictured in your mind. I gave up making New Year's resolutions years ago because I had never successfully kept a single one of them. But I now understand why. The word "resolution" comes from the root word "resolute," which means "admirably purposeful, determined, and unwavering." Most of us start out purposeful and determined, but the unwavering part comes only in the doing. The unwavering part keeps us from surrendering the resolution altogether. It is, in fact, our wavering that leads to quitting.

The first problem with my resolutions was that they were driven by motivation, as are many goals in life. When my motivation wavered, so did my resolve. It's easy to push through when your motivation is strong; it's much harder to continue when your motivation is at zero. And, because feelings drive motivation ("I feel like doing it" or "I don't feel like doing it") and our feelings change, our motivations are inconsistent, too. Take, for example, eating healthy. After the holiday indulgences, when our clothes no longer fit, we are motivated to make healthy choices. And for a few days or weeks, we do, but as soon as our clothes feel comfortable again, it is harder to continue to

⁙ Resolute Resolutions ⁘

choose healthy eating because our motivation (fitting into our clothes) is no longer a driving force. The taste of potato chips or ice cream becomes a stronger motivation than being healthy.

The same is true of our faith journeys. Have you ever noticed that most often, when God asks us to do something, it seems impossible? We find examples throughout Scripture—Abraham was supposed to be the father of many nations, but he was old and had no children; Moses was supposed to speak publicly, but he had a speech problem; Joseph was supposed to be an influential leader, but he was sold into slavery; the Israelites were supposed to capture a city by silently walking in circles; David was supposed to be king, but he was a mere shepherd boy; Mary was supposed to have a baby when she'd never slept with a man. I can only imagine their feelings wavering as they tried to believe in the face of reality. God spoke, but life didn't match up with what He said.

So, what do we do? How do we overcome our feelings and actually accomplish the things He has called us to do—even those that seem completely impossible? It turns out that the impossible is often the first step to deeper faith. But it isn't simply belief that brings us to see God do the impossible. Instead, He calls us to act, to step out in faith. Zechariah says we are to "finish the task." That first step in doing what seems impossible at the moment is how we begin to take heart. It forces us to draw on His strength and ultimately enables us to finish the task.

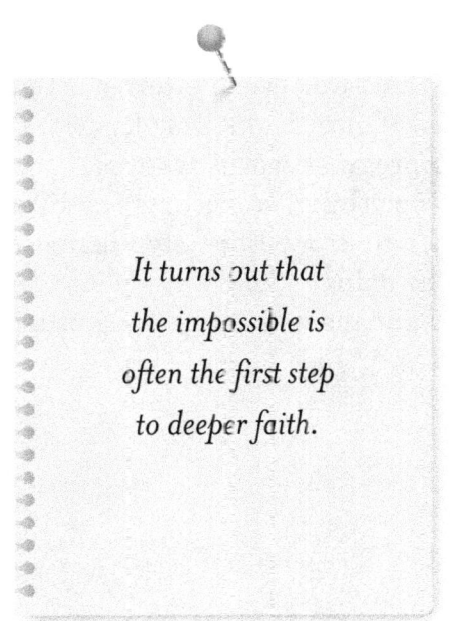

*It turns out that the impossible is often the first step to deeper faith.*

Simply thinking about the impossible task or

~ DISCIPLINE ~

problem with no solution only leads to feelings of inadequacy and fear, and we become overwhelmed. The longer we remain in this state, each has a deeper outcome—feeling inadequate paralyzes us, fear becomes anxiety, and being overwhelmed leads us into despair. So if motivation is inconsistent and keeps us from doing, but doing is the first step, how can we ever be resolute? It's really basic—start smaller. Eliminate the wavering motivation by starting with goals that don't depend on it. Find something that you *can* do that is so basic there is no excuse *not* to do it.

Let me give you a personal example: God has called me to write, but the idea of writing a book seemed so far beyond what I could do with my limited resources (time, skill, influence, etc.) that I spent years feeling inadequate and being frozen, doing nothing. To change my life's trajectory, I had to find a goal that wasn't motivated by my feelings but rather by my obedience. What could I do that would eliminate the excuses and help me take that first step? Write one sentence! If I had a long day or a bad day, could I write one sentence before going to bed? Yes! So, it started there. Once I had enough successes under my belt, writing more than one sentence became easier. Many nights, I wrote a paragraph or a page (which was even better), but I met my goal every day: one sentence. Once the habit is formed, the goal can be stretched, and our progress moves faster.

When we step out and do something, our hearts are lifted, and our faith is given a chance to grow. Each step brings us closer to finishing the task. The doing is how we take our tiny plants of faith out of the closet and place them in the Sonlight.

*It is our wavering
that leads to quitting...
because our feelings change,
our motivations
are inconsistent, too.*

# Map Your Journey

Think about your life for a moment. Do you struggle when your motivation is low? Are you inconsistent when you try to move forward? As you read through the options below and choose one or two to complete, try to keep your focus on starting small.

## *Journal Prompts*

- How often do feelings of inadequacy, fear, and being overwhelmed stop you from moving forward? What is one step you can take to push past your feelings?
- What was the last step of faith that you took? How did it turn out?
- What is one thing that you can do which will move you toward a deeper connection with God, regardless of your motivation?

## *Deeper Study*

- **Living in Faith**
  Philippians 2:14–16, 4:4–9; Hebrews 11:1–6
- **Start Small**
  1 Samuel 17:40; Zechariah 4:10; Matthew 13:31–32; Luke 16:10
- **Biblical Examples**
  Genesis 18:1–15 & 21:1–7; Genesis 37 & 41:37–57; Exodus 3:1–4:7; Joshua 6; 1 Samuel 16:1–13 & 2 Samuel 5:1–5; Luke 1:26–56

## Our Model

God asked Jesus to do the impossible—voluntarily surrender His perfect life for the penalty of the world. He wrestled with it, too. Read Luke 22:41–44. This passage paints an intense picture of Jesus' struggle in the garden shortly before His arrest. Imagine for a moment the impact on the world if Jesus had surrendered to His lack of motivation. Now reflect on the impact God may want to make on the world through your resolute obedience. When Jesus was struggling to stay strong, what happened? Are you willing to let God do that for you? Be honest in your prayers when your resolve is weak, and He will.

## Prayer

*"Prayer is a dialogue, not a monologue."*
—David Yonggi Cho

# The Taproot

*"But when you pray, go away by yourself, shut the door behind you, and pray to your Father in private. Then your Father, who sees everything, will reward you."*

—Matthew 6:6

As we move into the idea of specific spiritual disciplines, we will continue to look at some concepts that pertain to trees and their growth. In the first chapter of Part 1, I mentioned that the taproot is a tree's first root whose primary purpose is to seek out water. When we enter into a relationship with Jesus, Living Water is what we find in our prayer for salvation. It allows our seed of faith to sprout, and we find a source of Life, but one drink is not enough. God designed us with an insatiable thirst for more of Him which leads us on a deeper quest for water. Prayer is the taproot that maps our way.

But let's be honest; prayer is initially self-absorbed. It's about our own salvation. Many Christians continue to use their initial prayer of salvation as their model: ask God to do something and say thank you when He does it. But if you've been walking with Jesus for any time at all, you know that sometimes when we ask Him to do something, He doesn't. When that happens, the model we built for prayer falls apart.

This breakdown is why Jesus gave us a different way to pray. He did not teach us self-focused prayer but God-focused prayer. The Lord's Prayer is probably the most notable example, and for years it didn't occur to me that Scripture recorded other prayers of Jesus. We will always learn better and grow more deeply when we learn from Jesus Himself. He is the perfect example for us in all situations, and we can trust that His counsel is sound!

I'll be honest—I've always struggled with prayer. In my heart of hearts, I know that God hears our prayers, that He is a miracle-working God, and that He wants the best for each of us. I've seen Him perform miracles of healing, salvation, and life change time and again. But that enemy, oh how he tries to convince me that I am the exception—that my prayers are weak and have no impact.

I am not the exception. You are not. When we realize that prayer isn't a letter to Santa asking for what we want, when the truth of prayer gets down deep in our hearts, that's when everything changes. See, prayer has very little to do with asking God to grant our desires, even the "good" ones, and everything to do with strengthening our relationships with the Lord.

Picture for a moment the person to whom you are closest. Think about the conversations you have. What do they look like? How often do you talk and connect? That's the model for prayer. If you only asked for their help or for them to give you things, your relationship most likely wouldn't last very long; consumer friendships rarely do. If you only talk to them once a week, once a month, or once a year, they wouldn't remain the closest person in your life. But even though we do that with God far too often, He hasn't given up on us. He hasn't walked away. He's still trying to help us walk closer with Him. What deep love He has for us—and what divine patience!

The more we pray, the more we pray. It is so basic

> *Prayer has very little to do with asking God to grant our desires... and everything to do with strengthening our relationships with the Lord.*

and yet so hard. We must choose to pray. There are passing thought prayers throughout our day, "Lord, protect her," that we use, but the prayer of the righteous that is powerful and produces incredible results (James 5:16) doesn't look like that. It is not a quick text to God; it's time that we carve out for deep and meaningful conversations. It's a committed relationship that we prioritize.

In modern society, we have overwhelming options for communication, each with varying degrees of responsibility and commitment. There are social media "likes," texts, emails, phone calls, coffee dates, distraction-free dinners, and middle-of-the-night, pour-out-your-heart connection points; all of these can reflect the quality of our communication with our heavenly Father. He longs for the intimate, interruption-free connection of 2 a.m. conversations, but it doesn't start there; no relationship does. Building vulnerability and trust takes time. So it is with our prayer life. Difficulties, challenges, and adversity bring us closer together in our human relationships, and those same struggles can bring us closer to God. Or they can drive us away depending on how deep our roots go.

## Map Your Journey

As we look at our human relationships, we can often see where our communication is thriving or lacking. Before you jump into mapping your journey today, take a moment to reflect on your communication with the Lord.

### Journal Prompts

- How have you viewed prayer in the past? What is God showing you now?
- In what areas do you feel that your prayer life is thriving? In what areas is it lacking?
- Evaluate the deepness of your communication with God. Are you "liking" His posts on the Bible app? Do you send Him quick texts with your immediate needs? Do you write long emails full of detail and then run out of time to read His responses? Do you have regular "date nights" when He is your focus, and you are His? How do you want to see your communication with God deepen?

### Deeper Study

- **How to Pray**
  Matthew 6:5–15; Luke 18:9–14; James 5:13–18
- **Prayers of Jesus**
  Luke 3:21–22; John 11:41–43
- **Intimacy with God**
  Psalms 42:1–2, 139:1-24; James 4:8–10

## Our Model

When we talk about prioritizing our time with God, it is crucial to look at the life of Jesus. He inarguably had more demands, expectations, and responsibilities put on Him than we can imagine. Yet, despite those pressures, He prioritized His relationship with His Father. Read the verses below and reflect on how you can learn from His example. Ask the Holy Spirit to show you how to place a higher value on developing intimacy with God.

- Matthew 14:23
- Mark 1:35
- Luke 5:15–16; 6:12

# Gratitude

*Jesus said, "This is how you should pray: 'Father, may your name be kept holy. May your Kingdom come soon.'"*

—Luke 11:2

Gratitude is more than simply saying, "thank you." Oh, we can say the words and even mean them, but a grateful heart is most often born from an undeserved blessing. When we think we've earned something or deserve it, we are polite and express gratitude, but that doesn't go much deeper than good manners. Think about it for a moment; what are you most thankful for in your life? Now, ask yourself, "Why that over everything else?"

Deep gratitude may be difficult for those who are blessed and have never really had to do without something. Adults whose families struggled financially when they were growing up are often abundantly grateful for a steady income. People who lost a parent at a young age? Their hearts radiate joy and gratitude for every milestone they get to celebrate with their own childen. This is the way of gratitude: the more you do without, the more you appreciate.

Our gratitude toward God can vary as well. Still, I have found that those who genuinely take the time to understand and appreciate the blessings of adoption and citizenship find that gratitude organically grows and develops in their hearts. When gratitude fills our hearts, it isn't hidden; it overflows as praise and adoration. We long to honor the one who blessed us.

Whether we had terrific parents, no parents, or people posing as parents, not one of us had a perfect parent. We each had human parents (or parent models). Because of this, we have all experienced hurt from our families. When we find Christ, Scripture tells us that God adopts us into His family (Ephesians 1:5). It's why we get to call Him Abba Father. At that moment, He not only takes us from whatever human family experience we have had, but He also calls us His own and makes us His son or daughter!

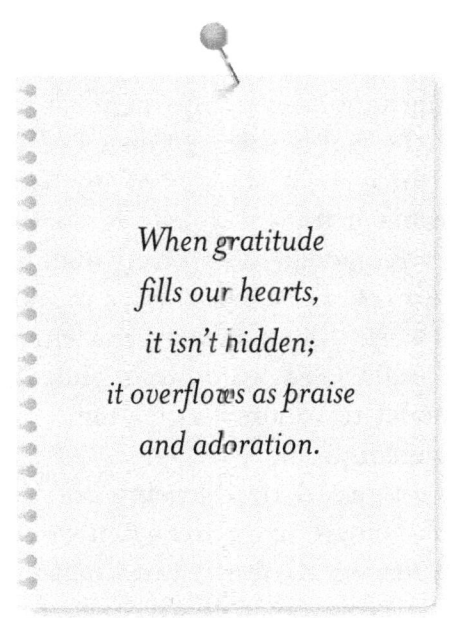

*When gratitude fills our hearts, it isn't hidden; it overflows as praise and adoration.*

Because of Christ's redemptive work on the cross, our Father begins a DNA transfusion, removing our sinful human cells and replacing them with His righteous supernatural ones. The Holy Spirit is the One who leads us through this lifelong treatment plan. However, there will be a day when sin is no more, a day when we will fully resemble our perfect Father because we will finally be in remission from sin!

When I think about my past—my mistakes, my sin, the times I've hurt others (especially those I love)—I feel unworthy of bearing His Name, of being His daughter. At that moment, my heart swells and my eyes fill because the gratitude is so intense. I do not deserve to be His daughter, and there is certainly nothing I have done to earn adoption, yet I am His! What blessing and what joy my heart finds in that truth.

Another miracle that brings a clearer perspective is citizenship. We go from being slaves of our enemy to citizens of a Kingdom we have yet to see. It's like being born abroad but knowing where we truly belong. When the customs and ideologies of the place in which we reside don't make sense and leave us feeling like fish out of water, we can begin to understand why. This place is not our home! We are spiritual beings having

~ PRAYER ~

a human experience, not the other way around. Since it's not our nationality it's not supposed to feel comfortable.

So why does understanding our citizenship increase our gratitude? Because we get all the rights and privileges of our heavenly citizenship, which include the protection of our King. When things here feel unbearable or unfair, we can remember that we are citizens of another Kingdom. When we finish our work as ambassadors, we get to go *Home*. We don't have to adopt the patterns or customs of this world—fear, anxiety, insecurity, comparison. We get to live under the guidelines that He established, and we get to model to others the customs and characteristics of our real citizenship.

Yet somehow, we quickly forget all the blessings of God when we feel that things aren't going our way or when we are walking through a challenging season. It's pretty presumptuous to expect someone to be at our beck and call when we don't appreciate them. Yet He is always right there, no matter how we treat Him. Not because we are entitled to the relationship but because His love for us is that great. We ought to love Him back and take time every day to thank Him for who He is and all He does for us.

As we get to know Him, it is essential to learn who He is straight from Scripture and not from our own ideologies or worldviews. The more we understand His character, the more grateful we become. In Hebrew, the word Jehovah means "I AM THAT I AM"; it is the name God gave when Moses asked who he should say had sent him to the Israelites (Exodus 3:13–15). There are multiple times

> *The more we understand His character, the more grateful we become.*

36

when Scripture pairs the word Jehovah with another word to describe the character of God. Because of these combined words, we know He is:

- **Jehovah Jireh—God who Provides**
  Genesis 22:1–18
- **Jehovah Rapha—God who Heals**
  Exodus 15:22–26; 2 Kings 20:1–6
- **Jehovah Nissi—God my Banner** (He fights for me)
  Exodus 17:8–16
- **Jehovah Shalom—God my Peace**
  Judges 6:11–24
- **Jehovah Raah—God my Shepherd**
  Psalm 23:1–4
- **Jehovah Tsidkenu—God our Righteousness**
  Jeremiah 23:1–6, 33:14–26

## Map Your Journey

When Jesus teaches us to pray in Luke 11:2, we see acknowledgment of our adoption (addressing God as Father), we realize that we should give honor to Him (may Your name be kept holy), and we understand that have citizenship not of this earth (may Your kingdom come soon). Before you begin to map your journey today, pause and let gratitude spring up in your heart simply because of who He is.

### *Journal Prompts*

- When you consider being adopted by a perfect Father, what feelings surface? Write a prayer expressing your gratitude.
- When traveling, it is often apparent who the natives are, who the immigrants are, and who the tourists are. When the world sees you, do they easily identify you as a native, an immigrant, or an ambassador of His Kingdom?
- Think about what you need from God right now and select one of the names of God from this chapter. Read the story surrounding that particular name and write down any keywords, phrases, or imagery that encourages you.

### *Deeper Study*

- **Gratitude and Praise**
  Psalms 9:1, 100:4–5; Daniel 2:19–23; Revelation 4:11
- **Adoption**
  Romans 8:14–17; Ephesians 1:5; 1 Peter 1:3–6
- **Citizenship**
  Philippians 3:17–21; Hebrews 13:14; Revelation 21:1–4

## Our Model

In Matthew 11:25–29, we read a prayer of thanksgiving that Jesus prayed. As you read it, consider what He is actually thanking God for. Don't just read the words He says; look at the heart behind them, paying attention to verse 26. Reflect on your prayers of gratitude. What is most often the focus (i.e., blessings He's given you, His character, His purpose, etc.)?

# Repentance

*"...And forgive us our sins, as we forgive those who sin against us. And don't let us yield to temptation."*

—Luke 11:4

I want to challenge you with something today. We refer to Jesus as our Lord and Savior but often equate the two descriptions as the same. The expression isn't redundant. When we come to faith, Jesus becomes our Savior; when we surrender control of our lives, He becomes our Lord. For some people that happens simultaneously; for others, there are two separate and distinct moments. I want you to understand this because we need to realize that repentance is ultimately about surrender.

Nothing we say to others has real meaning if it's not sincere. Forgiveness is not about saying you're sorry. It involves more than words; it requires both confession and repentance. Confession is our admission of guilt, while repentance is our remorse for it. Confessing our mistakes, sins, fears, pain, weaknesses, and being remorseful for hurting God and others is the way to ensure that our hearts are in the right place and our motives remain pure.

**Mistakes**—Sometimes, we just make a poor choice. Not acknowledging it and not asking God's forgiveness when we rush ahead of Him charts a course that leads straight to sin. As soon as we realize the error, we need to own it and change direction.

**Sins**—Sometimes, our bad choices are outright disobedience to God. Once we arrive at that place, we need to realize how much it hurts Him. Our sorrow for hurting Him leads to repentance and a desire to better show our love for Him.

**Fears**—His Word teaches us that fear is not from Him, so we should do everything we can to be free from it. Anxiety is fear on steroids. If we learn to take our thoughts captive before they develop into full-blown scenarios, we can learn to become masters over fear and anxiety rather than remaining slaves to them.

**Pain**—This life is full of hurts, and they can become like cinder blocks weighing us down. Unforgiveness is the mortar that cements these blocks, creating a wall. Constructing a wall around our hearts doesn't protect us the way we think it will. Instead, it creates a barrier between us and others—between us and God. The only way to have an open heart is to allow Him to tear down the wall and bring healing to our pain.

**Weaknesses**—We aren't perfect, and He doesn't want or expect us to be. Some people struggle with the pride of thinking they have no weaknesses, and others struggle with the pride of thinking they shouldn't have weaknesses. Realizing and confessing our weaknesses is essential for everyone. Owning our shortcomings rather than using them as excuses brings us to a place of humility.

> *When we are genuinely repentant, it builds an unavoidable humility in us.*

When we are genuinely repentant, it builds an unavoidable humility in us. We admit that we are wrong. We own that it is our fault. We surrender our pride. Many of us struggle to do this, yet when we focus on the reality that God is not angry with us and that He is our safe sanctuary, we can come to

Him with remorseful humility, confident in His love, and His willingness to forgive. Forgiveness for our sins comes after they are confessed to the One we've offended—our Father. Sometimes our sin isn't just against Him; sometimes we hurt others. When that happens, we must make our confession to all offended parties.

Because God freely forgives us, He instructs us to freely forgive others. That certainly isn't easy and deserves a chapter of its own, so we will go into that more when we talk later about community. For now, I want to focus on surrendering the pain to God through confession. Before we can forgive someone else, it helps to allow God to heal us from our wounds. Many churches offer a Freedom ministry which can be a catalyst for healing; I have been able to participate in several, and here's what I've learned: we often want to say, "I forgive you," and move on, but like an apology, the words aren't enough. People hurt us in varying degrees, but the process for healing is really the same. We can't just say, "so-and-so hurt me; I forgive them," and expect the pain to disappear. We must slow down and bring it to the Lord.

Often, the pain isn't even what we see on the surface. When we submit the situation in prayer, the Holy Spirit can peel back the layers and expose the root. Minor scratches often hurt more than they should because they were inflicted on a part of the heart that already had a deeper injury, maybe one that has been infected a long time. Once we understand where the real pain is coming from, it's also important to confess to the Lord how we genuinely feel about it. I struggle with this because I am an emotional person and don't want to relive those feelings. It hurt enough the first time! While we think stuffing it away is less painful, any infection that goes untreated will fester. I have found that God's healing touch is most powerful when I invite Him into my pain. His presence is a balm that soothes and comforts in a way no one else can. Acknowledging the emotions associated with the offense may reveal a familiar feeling—failure, rejection, inadequacy, abandonment, etc. The repeated feeling generally points to the source of a festering wound. When God heals that deeper laceration, the scratches go back to being scratches that heal easier, and we recover more quickly.

Remember, He lets us choose. Always. We can choose humility and repentance, or we can choose pride and sin. We can choose to let Him heal our hearts, or we can choose to live with the heartbreaking disease of unforgiveness. Surrender is a choice.

## Map Your Journey

Biblical repentance recognizes the problem. It takes responsibility for the pain it causes the Lord, others, and us, and asks God to restore what the enemy stole from us. When we walk through repentance in our prayer time, it is vital not only to confess and seek forgiveness but also to ask the Holy Spirit to fill the now empty space in our hearts with His fruit (Galatians 5:22–23) and the void in our minds with the truth from His Word (Romans 12:2). Practice that today as you select one or two of the items below to walk through with the Lord.

### *Journal Prompts*

- In what areas are you making mistakes that could lead to a pattern of sin? Reflect on how those mistakes impact your relationships with others (including God!) and write out a prayer of confession.
- Make a list of the things that are currently causing you to feel fearful or anxious. Then, write out the verses that speak His truth over them. Read and pray these verses daily for the next week.
- Is there anyone in your life who has hurt you and the pain is still throbbing? Before confessing it to the Lord, take some time and write down who hurt you, what they did, and how it made you feel. That last part is essential because it helps you identify exactly where you need the Lord's healing touch. After you finish, prayerfully confess your pain to the Lord and ask for His healing. Repeat as needed.

### Deeper Study

- **Sin**
  Psalm 32:1–5; Isaiah 1:18; Acts 3:19–20;
  Colossians 3:5–10
- **Fear/Anxiety**
  Psalm 34:4–5; Isaiah 43:1–2; Luke 12:22–26;
  2 Timothy 1:7
- **Unforgiveness**
  Proverbs 24:17–18; Matthew 6:14–15; Mark 11:25;
  Luke 17:3–4

### Our Model

We must remember that our Father is a safe sanctuary even in the storms created by our foolishness or lack of faith. Read the accounts found in Matthew 14:22–32 and John 8:1–11. As you read take note of how Jesus responds, His words and actions, to both Peter's fear and the woman publicly caught in her sin. How do His responses apply to you?

# Requests

*"Give us each day the food we need..."*

—LUKE 11:3

Needs and wants run a fine line nowadays, and an entitled worldview has led us to a deeper confusion that can trip us up in our prayers. Because we can't always tell the difference, we must learn how to focus our prayers more on the fulfillment of God's will and less on our own desires. God knows what we need, and He knows His will, so when we come to Him with our petitions, we must be humble and mindful of His Sovereignty. That doesn't mean we don't ask, but asking with humility means learning to ask for His will and surrendering ours. This is not easy. We want to escape pain, hardship, and struggle, but this prideful approach does not help us grow. If anyone deserved an easy life, it was the perfect Son of God. If He didn't have one while on this earth, what makes us think we are entitled to one?

Another stumbling block we too often create when bringing our requests to the Father is double-mindedness; we want the best of both worlds. We ask God for two contradictory things, like:

- Stop their suffering; also, don't let them die.
- Make my faith stronger; also, protect me from bad things happening.
- Teach me patience; also, remove annoying people from my life.

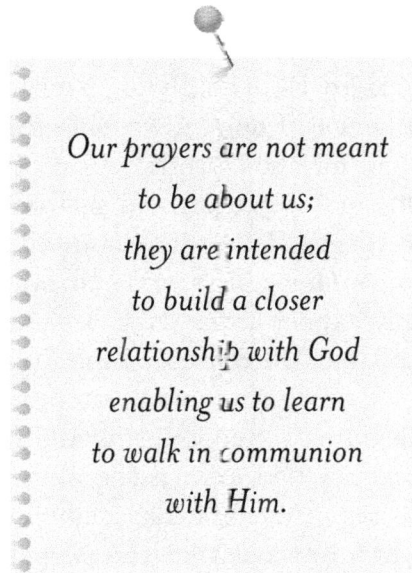

*Our prayers are not meant to be about us; they are intended to build a closer relationship with God enabling us to learn to walk in communion with Him.*

When we double-side our prayers, we set God up to look like 1) He doesn't answer, or 2) He does whatever we want. Neither is correct. God cannot be manipulated. Jesus taught us to pray with a single-minded focus when He prayed in the Garden of Gethsemane "...I want your will to be done, not mine" (Mark 14:36). Letting go of what we want isn't easy, but it is crucial to our spiritual growth.

Our prayers are not meant to be about us; they are intended to build a closer relationship with God enabling us to learn to walk in communion with Him. When we focus our prayers on what we think is best, we can miss the abundance God has planned.

I like surprises. I know not everyone does, and I honestly can't understand that. I love knowing something amazing is coming and the thrill of anticipation leading up to it. I've always been that way—Christmas, birthdays, surprise trips, unexpected gifts. All of the "guess what?" moments in life trigger a childlike joy in me.

A perfect example was my twenty-fifth wedding anniversary. My husband planned something for us to do and asked if I wanted to know what it was. My passionate reply? "Absolutely not!" He did tell me the day before that we were flying somewhere, but I did not know where until we arrived at the gate. Even then, I knew our destination but not what adventures were to come. Every moment he had planned, every step, every car ride, the entire weekend, felt like an extended Christmas morning experience of opening one package after another. I will never forget that trip because it was beyond anything I had expected or imagined.

The Bible teaches us to come to God boldly and with a spirit of expectation. But, if I'm honest, I don't always do that. Why? Because I don't want to ask for the "wrong" thing. If I come to Him asking for miracles and supernatural victories, and He chooses not to do those things, I am disappointed or hurt. Those feelings aren't because God didn't come through; they are because I didn't align my expectations with His plan. When I brought this struggle to God, He reminded me of my anniversary trip to New York City. My excitement stemmed from having no idea of what was going to happen. It would not have been nearly as joyful for me if I had known the plan. It would have been good, but not the same. My childlike excitement came from the surprise. I only had to trust that the surprise was good. This excitement is our boldness of expectation, and trusting Him is our act of humility.

Do you know that all of God's plans for us are good? That the only surprises He plans are worth it? When we fully recognize His goodness and His love for us, it enables us to come to Him in prayer with that same excitement of, "Where are we going? I can't wait to find out!" Yes, bad things happen in this life, but His surprise for us today is what He will do in the middle of it. And after it. And when the next adventure comes.

When we shift our focus from what we want to what we need, we find ourselves seeking His provision above all else. The NIV translation of this verse reads, "Give us each day our daily bread." While bread is nourishment for our bodies, Jesus Himself is the Bread of Life (John 6:32–35); we ought to daily ask for both physical and spiritual nourishment. When we focus on seeking His provision for today, it simplifies all of our requests and removes any doubt about whether or not He will answer us. Providing for His children is always His will; the anticipation is found in the surprise of "how."

Understanding the difference between needs and wants causes a shift in our prayer lives. We find ourselves asking for less "stuff" and for our character to grow. We worry less about the timing of His answer because we learn that it takes time for His character traits to develop in us. Jesus walked so closely with His Father that He knew His perfect will in every situation. As we walk closer to Him, we can also grow in our knowledge of His will.

## Map Your Journey

Before you read through today's options, think about your prayer requests. Do you find yourself asking God for your own specific agenda, or is your heart open to the leading of His Spirit?

### Journal Prompts

- We can ask God for anything. He knows our hearts, and He knows our levels of faith. What have you been afraid to ask for? Why? Consider whether it is a want or a need. How can you ask with His will as the focus?
- What plans are you holding on to that God may be asking you to let go of? Is it a relationship? A job? A dream? Write about it and then complete the Deeper Study below on "God's Will."
- If you need to shift from self-focused prayers to God-focused, what are one or two practical ways you can practice surrendering your plans for His?

### Deeper Study

- **Asking God**
  Luke 11:9–13; John 12:27–28, 15:16; 1 John 5:14–15
- **God's Promises**
  Proverbs 3:5–6; Isaiah 43:18–19; Romans 8:28–30; Philippians 1:6
- **God's Will**
  1 Thessalonians 5:18; 1 Timothy 2:3–4; Hebrews 13:20–21; 2 Peter 3:9

## *Our Model*

Jesus struggled with wanting to submit to God's will, too. He even asked God for something He knew wasn't part of His plan. The difference? He was honest about how He felt and yet willing to let go of His momentary desire so He could accomplish God's purpose. Read Matthew 26:36–44. What phrases resonate with you? If you have prayed similar prayers, think about the outcomes. Like Christ, did you ultimately surrender, or did you stubbornly hold on to wanting your own way. How did those situations end?

# Listen

*"My sheep listen to my voice; I know them, and they follow me."*
—John 10:27

In the last chapter, we talked about asking God for our needs during our prayer time. Today we're going to talk about letting Him speak. Many things can destroy a marriage, but lack of communication is on the top of the list. It is important to remember that communication is speaking, listening, and receiving—by both parties. When a relationship lacks healthy communication, it's like a tree without water. First, its growth is stunted, but too long without water and it will die. Our relationships with God work the same way. If the taproot never goes deep enough to find a water source, the tiny sprout withers and dies.

Remember, prayer can't only be a quick text we send God; it's time we carve out for deep and meaningful conversation. Now, don't misunderstand me; all communication with God is good. Something is always better than nothing. But if you want deep roots, communication has to be ongoing, and it has to be two-way. It always

> *Remember, prayer can't only be a quick text we send God; it's time we carve out for deep and meaningful conversation.*

surprises me when someone shares their failed attempt to have deep, meaningful conversations via text. As a professional communicator, I strongly advocate for these conversations to be face-to-face. We lose too much in a text—tone, eye contact, emotion (although fun, emojis do not qualify). Things like conflict resolution, dreaming, and connecting need to happen in person. You show me a friendship that communicates only by text, and I'll show you a relationship that won't last, especially one that depends on deep intimacy, like a marriage.

So, our pop-up prayers, those quick texts to God, are good, but they aren't enough. We need to treat Him with the respect and tenderness we show in any valuable relationship. He loves to know when we think about Him during the day and to share those quick moments with us, but He also desires dinnertime connection and pillow talk, date nights and weekend getaways. It's essential to prioritize our prayer time the same way we do our other relationships. We must make room for Him and create space to listen. The margin may look different for each of us depending on our seasons in life. You may have more "stolen" moments if you have young children. If you're young and single, you may have hour-long walks in a park every night. For those in a more seasoned stage of life, the routine may be more scheduled and predictable.

In all my years of walking alongside women in our faith journeys, one of the most common questions is, "How do I know if it's God speaking or just me?" It doesn't matter how long you've been following Christ; we all worry that we will mishear Him. What's so funny is that it's much harder than you think to misunderstand God. He speaks to us in so many ways—the Bible, sermons, worship, circumstances, people, creation—that we can be reassured and have confirmation in any situation. So why do we worry so much? Isaiah 30:21 teaches us that we can hear Him with our own ears. It tells us that His voice is with us, guiding us in the way we should go and directing every step if we listen. The hard part is that we have to slow down and stop talking.

~ PRAYER ~

When I served in Children's Ministry, kids asked about knowing God's voice, too. My response to them was a question, "Is it something you want to do?" Most of the time, the answer was "no." Well, if it isn't something we want to do (forgive someone, give generously, etc.), then there is a strong possibility that it's the Holy Spirit speaking. That's one filter. We must ask an essential second question, "Does it contradict His Word or His character?" If the answer is "yes," then it is NOT the Holy Spirit speaking to us.

When my husband and I met, you couldn't have found two more opposite people. We didn't agree on much of anything. So, we learned early in our marriage that when we agreed we knew it was God. Every decision we've made over the years has been one made in unity. If we prayed and heard different answers, we knew one of us was missing it. So we would go back and pray some more. God will not give two believers different answers to the same question. When our daughter was in high school and had to start making decisions for her future, we applied the same principle as a family. We all sought God's guidance regarding what college she should attend, the program God led her to pursue, and even where to apply to graduate school. For each of these significant decisions, God confirmed the same thing for each of us. It wasn't always the first time; sometimes, we had to go back and ask again, but we all found peace with the same answer in the end. This type of accountability is beneficial when you are learning to listen to God's voice. It isn't simply asking someone's opinion; it's

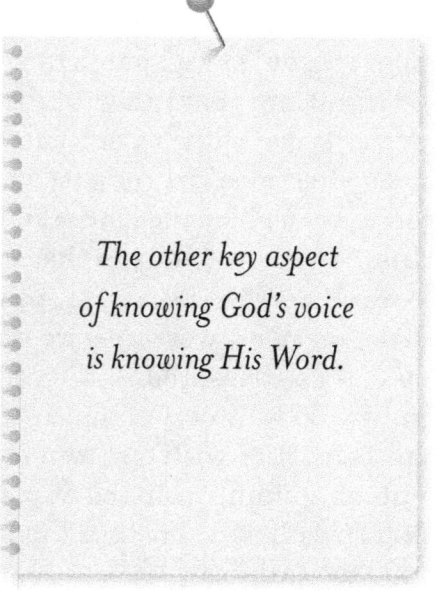

*The other key aspect of knowing God's voice is knowing His Word.*

asking them to partner with you in prayer until you agree on what you hear.

The other key aspect of knowing God's voice is knowing His Word. We learn His character, promises, instructions, and even His plans for us through His Word. We will dive deeper into the spiritual discipline of knowing His Word in the next section, so get ready!

## Map Your Journey

Not all of us are naturally good listeners. Even those who are can still struggle when overwhelmed, anxious, or distracted. Listening to God is something we can all grow in, so take a moment before moving on to stop and pray. Don't speak—just listen.

### *Journal Prompts*

- Recognizing God's voice takes time. When a stranger calls your name, you don't recognize the voice, but you still turn and look. What are you doing to get to know His voice better? What are some action steps you could take this week?
- Are you more of a talker or a listener? How does this help you in your prayer life? How might it hinder you? What do you think the Holy Spirit might be teaching you about listening?
- Two-way communication leads to a healthy relationship. What can you change today to make your communication with the Lord more substantial and your relationship healthier?
- If the idea of a deep and meaningful conversation with the Lord seems incomprehensible to you, take a few moments to reflect on what those conversations look like within your human relationships. Jot down some key things that come to mind and consider that while Jesus is fully God, He was also fully human. How can you apply those same human relationship principles to your prayer life?

### Deeper Study

- **God Speaks**
  1 Kings 19:11–13; Isaiah 55:11; Jeremiah 33:3; 2 Peter 1:20–21
- **We Listen**
  Isaiah 30:21; Matthew 7:24–27; Hebrews 3:15
- **Connection**
  Psalm 85:8; Zephaniah 3:17; John 15:1–27

### Our Model

In John chapter 10, Jesus teaches the importance of hearing His voice and how it impacts our relationships with Him. Read verses 1–30 and consider what it means to be a sheep led by a Good Shepherd. Take a moment to pray and ask the Holy Spirit to speak to you. Ask Him to help you hear His voice, then write out whatever comes to mind. Do the words and phrases align with His Word and His character? What tone did that voice have? If you aren't sure, reach out to a Christian friend and work through it together.

# Persistence

*Faith shows the reality of what we hope for; it is the evidence of things we cannot see.*

—Hebrews 11:1

We have a faith problem in the American church when it comes to prayer. We don't want to admit it, or maybe we don't realize it, but we do. Here is what I mean: we believe that God can, but we aren't as quick to believe that He will. It doesn't necessarily start that way, but more often than we want to admit, it is where we end up.

Can God save those family members who are so very far from Him? Absolutely! Will He? It's possible, but it really is a matter of their hearts. When we first begin to pray, our hearts are full of faith, "God, I know you love them more than I do. I know they are your children, and you want them to come home. Surround them with believers, and soften their hearts to your Spirit. Let them find You, Lord." How long do we pray that way? Weeks, months, maybe a year or two. At some point, to mask our disappointment, we find ourselves saying things like, "God's timing is perfect," or "sometimes people just choose rebellion." Our faith in what we had hoped for is no longer certain about what we do not see.

A lack of healing, a lost loved one, an opportunity that doesn't come—these are all examples of times when we let go of faith. Hebrews doesn't tell us to have faith for two years or that God only listens to the prayer the first 100 times. Faith is something God calls us to have always, even when we see no sign of the miracle, even *more so* when we see no sign of the miracle.

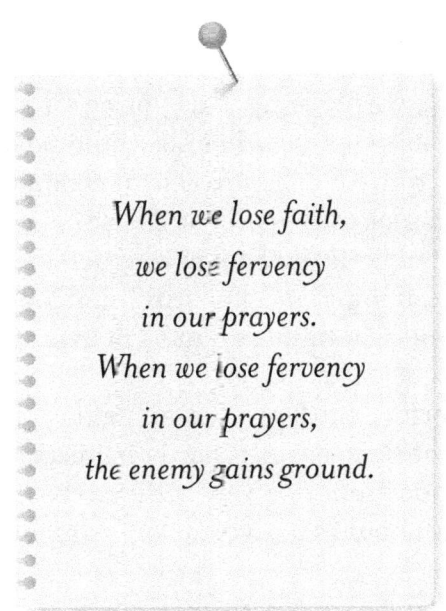

*When we lose faith, we lose fervency in our prayers. When we lose fervency in our prayers, the enemy gains ground.*

Sometimes people aren't healed. Sometimes loved ones don't find Jesus. It's hard to have faith when there is that doubt of "What if He doesn't?" But that is not how God desires us to live our lives; that is not walking in faith. It is not the standard God has set for us. When we lose faith, we lose fervency in our prayers. When we lose fervency in our prayers, the enemy gains ground. Spiritual warfare is very real. Battles are being fought between angels and demons that we do not see, battles for our souls and those we love. Our Spirit-filled prayers are one weapon to help in the fight, yet we lay them down when our faith gives out.

Many years ago, I had a best friend. She was honestly the friend I'd prayed for my whole life. There was one problem, she wasn't following Christ. I knew that God brought us into each other's lives for a purpose. We had amazing conversations about how Jesus wanted to be her best friend, how He could heal her marriage, and how much He loved her. I prayed for her constantly because I loved her so very much, and I was grateful to have her in my life. I couldn't imagine eternity without her. Then she betrayed me. In a blink, the friendship was over, and I was reeling. I grieved as though she had died, for in my heart, she had. I was deeply angry and beyond hurt. I stopped praying for her because I stopped caring.

But then God did something truly remarkable. She found Jesus, and she began to pray. For me! For our relationship to be healed and restored. I didn't know any of this until several years later when she reached out. I wish that I had been praying, too. It still breaks my heart how I responded, but God is so very faithful. The faith of my sworn enemy, this young Christ follower, was strong enough to ask God for what she could never see happening. Her bold prayers led to the miracle of complete restoration in our lives. She is not only my best friend; she is my beautiful sister in Christ. Our relationship is so much more than I could ever have hoped or imagined. I am still humbled to think that her faith was stronger than mine, and I'm grateful that God used it for my good.

I won't pretend I have perfect faith. I still struggle with being persistent sometimes, but God is consistently helping me grow even when I am not as consistent as I would like to be. He doesn't give up on us, so we shouldn't give up on ourselves either.

*Our Spirit-filled prayers
are one weapon
to help in the fight,
yet we lay them down
when our faith gives out.*

## Map Your Journey

Persistence requires both faith and discipline. Which one is easier for you? As you read through your options for today, look for one or two that will help strengthen the area where you need to grow.

### Journal Prompts

- Is there something that you have stopped believing God can or will do? How might He reawaken your faith in that area?
- Make a list of prayers not yet answered. This time as you pray don't ask God to change or fix something; ask for His will to be done. Ask for your character to grow as you wait and for restored hope in the miracle.
- When a prayer request goes unanswered, you may have heard someone say, "sometimes God's answer is no." Sometimes that's true. But there are other times the miracle doesn't happen because humans have free will. Make a list of prayers you believe weren't answered. Prayerfully release them to God and ask Him to restore your faith and belief that He is still a miracle-working Father.

### Deeper Study

- **Faith/Persistence**
  Psalm 116:1–2; Isaiah 40:27–31; Luke 18:1–8
- **Hope**
  Psalm 94:19; Romans 8:24–25, 12:12, 15:13
- **Intercession**
  Romans 15:30–32; Ephesians 1:16–20, 3:14–19; Philippians 1:9–11

## Our Model

The Bible records an intercessory prayer of Jesus in John 17:6–26. As you read it, look for specific things that He prayed for on behalf of others; take special note of how He prayed for you. This week, as you pray for your loved ones, imitate our Lord in how you pray.

# Part 3

## Scripture

*"Whatever keeps me from my Bible is my enemy,
however harmless it may appear to be."*

—A.W. Tozer

# The Root System

*Let your roots grow down into him, and let your lives be built on him Then your faith will grow strong in the truth you were taught, and you will overflow with thankfulness.*
—COLOSSIANS 2:7

If someone were to tell you that they had just finished reading a book on how to fly a plane and then invited you to be their passenger on a cross-country flight, what would you say? The phrase, "um... no," comes to mind! Why? Because knowledge and experience are not the same things. When talking with people about the next step on their faith journeys, it amazes me how many of them do not spend time reading God's Word. They know they should, and it will help them, but they don't. Why? Because knowledge and experience are not the same things. Until you take that step of faith, until you choose to embrace the things that will expand your root system, you do not have the experience you need.

We discussed in Part 2 how a taproot seeks out water. This section will look at how the root system develops, providing nutrients and the nourishment needed to grow. Our spiritual nutrition, and ultimately our growth, comes from the Word of God. Jesus teaches us in Matthew 4:4, "People do not live by bread alone, but on every word that comes from the mouth of God." His statement wasn't a new concept; He was quoting Deuteronomy 8:3. He reminded the Israelites of their history—of a time when they were drifting in the desert, wholly reliant on God for their nourishment. During that wilderness wandering adventure, God provided miraculous manna (bread)

## Scripture

that fell each day from heaven. Their job was to gather enough for that day and eat it while it was fresh. He still provides fresh nourishment for us daily, but we must consume it.

I'm going to be honest. This was me. It was more than twenty years before I started to understand what was missing in my relationship with God and why my roots were so weak and shallow that the slightest breeze would uproot me. I didn't even realize that my relationship with Him was stunted—that I wasn't getting the nutrients I needed. I was malnourished in my faith, which left me weakened and vulnerable.

Scripture teaches us that God's Word, the Bible, is living and active. What does that mean? It means that while unchanged, it is also fluid. With the help of the Holy Spirit, you can read the same verse today that you read five years ago, and God can show you something fresh and relevant about where you are in this moment. It means that you and your friend can be sitting in the same church service and walk away with entirely different perspectives on the same sermon. God is personal. He knows each of us individually; He knows our exact needs at any given moment. Because of this, we can approach His Word with excitement about what He will say to us today.

How do we take the knowledge we have and transfer it into a life-changing experience? There's only one step—we must choose to. Every day when we wake up, we have a choice: to obey or not. We have the option to either do what He wants or what we want; to spend time in Scripture or not. It seems so easy, so why is it so hard? Because there is an

> *If Satan can't steal our salvation, he wants to stunt our growth, and he will throw every excuse our way to do so.*

enemy of our souls who knows the life change that comes from spending time in God's Word. If Satan can't steal our salvation, he wants to stunt our growth, and he will throw every excuse our way to do so. The many battles he wages against us keep us from the Bible, but here's what I've learned—every excuse is a lie. The more I read the Truth, the more I can identify the lies. Let me show you:

- **I have a big day today, and I need extra sleep to be ready for it.** Nothing prepares us more for our day than time with God. It's prideful to think we can do it without Him. (John 15:5)
- **It's not that big of a deal to miss one day.** God is merciful and gracious, but He is a jealous God, and He desires time with us. It's idolatry to choose to put other things before Him. (James 4:4-8)
- **I love my bed.** Complacency and self-indulgence do not make us more like Christ. We know of times He even prayed through the night. (Luke 22:46)
- **I woke up late and will be late for work.** We have to cut something, but why Him instead of something else? When we put God first, He always sorts out the rest. (Matthew 6:33)
- **I have so much to do today; I don't have time.** When we prioritize our lives the way God instructs us, we have more time, energy, and rest. It's God-math: 2+2=whatever He wants it to be! (Proverbs 16:3)

## Map Your Journey

Take a few minutes to reflect on knowledge vs. experience. As you read through the prompts, select one or two that focus on where you need a few extra nutrients.

### Journal Prompts

- Do you find it easier to learn from your own mistakes (experience) or other people's (wisdom)? Why do you think that is? How does that help you? In what ways could you better balance the two?
- Write a few sentences describing your current root system. Is it deep? Expansive? Are your roots healthy and strong? Ask the Holy Spirit to show you any weakened or diseased areas.
- Where is your spiritual nourishment coming from right now? Are you slowing down to digest His Word or rushing through it like a drive-through order?

### Deeper Study

- **Wisdom**
  1 Corinthians 2:1–16; 2 Timothy 3:15–17; James 1:5–8, 3:13–18
- **Nutrition**
  Proverbs 4:20–23; John 4:31–34, 6:48–51
- **Growth**
  1 Corinthians 3:1–3; 1 Peter 2:1–3; 2 Peter 1:2–9

## *Our Model*

Knowledge without experience or understanding can be a dangerous thing. Pride in what you know can keep your mind from being open to what you don't. First, read Exodus 20:8, and then read Luke 6:1–11. Do you see how the Pharisees were more concerned with the letter of the law (immaturity) than the Spirit of it (maturity)? How does Jesus model the balance between head knowledge and heart knowledge for us?

# Healthy Digestion

*But Jesus told him, "No! The Scriptures say, 'People do not live by bread alone, but by every word that comes from the mouth of God.'"*
—MATTHEW 4:4

This story in the fourth chapter of Matthew drops us into a time when Jesus was vulnerable (verses 1–2) and tempted by Satan (verse 3). We often fail to recognize that our enemy knows God's Word. In this passage and others, it is apparent that He knows it and twists it. If we don't want to fall victim to Satan's deception, we must know God's Word better. In verse 6, Satan uses Psalm 91:11–12 (out of context) to tempt Jesus into choosing his plan over God's. Jesus doesn't hesitate to respond with Deuteronomy 6:16 (in context). Even with that, Satan doesn't stop. He attempts to appeal to Jesus' pride, but that doesn't work either. Three times Jesus responds with the Word of God, and the devil finally leaves Him alone until the next opportunity (Luke 4:13).

This passage taught me that when we don't consume the Word of God, we are spiritually starving. It is good to fast from the physical, but it is never good to fast from the spiritual. Although Jesus was without physical nourishment for 40 days, He had spent time with His Father. We know this because He remained strong when the spiritual battle came. If right now you feel weak in your life and lack the strength to keep going, I encourage you to make a list of what you're consuming.

Many doctors advise people with particular dietary issues to keep a log of what they're putting into their bodies as to help identify the source of their symptoms. If you are experiencing spiritual weakness, you can do the same. Keep a daily log for a week or two of everything your heart and your mind consume; include the quantity! Note things like social media, sermons, television, podcasts, movies, news broadcasts, conversations with others (be sure to note if they are life-giving or life-draining), God's Word, or anything else that impacts your spiritual health. Review the entries and calculate the amount of time spent ingesting things that sustain life versus the amount spent consuming the world's spiritual "junk food."

Any healthy diet ensures that nutrition is part of our eating plans. In the same way, we must consider the nutritional aspects of our spiritual diets; we must continue to consume every word that comes from the mouth of God. We accomplish this in our prayer time, the time we spend reading and studying Scripture, and the time we set aside to be in community with others who are on the same diet and can offer us healthy spiritual nourishment. These are the good foods of our spiritual sustenance. If we want to be healthier, we cut out food that isn't life-sustaining—refined sugar, processed foods, artificial sweeteners, fried food—we all know what they are.

Apply the same concept to spiritual health. If you look at your "food log," you can see what things are not from "the mouth of God." If you want to build your faith muscles to be in better shape when the enemy tempts you, then it's time to focus on your diet. Fast from the things that weaken your spirit and consume what strengthens you. The more you remove what is unhealthy and replace it with healthy choices, the more quickly you will see results. Starting small is certainly a start, but how soon do you want to see growth?

There are many ways that God speaks to us today—sermon messages, worship, circumstances, people, prayer, creation—but at the heart of each of these is the Bible. We must read, study, and memorize His Word. It is not always easy, but it is necessary for our transformation into the likeness of Christ. To model our lives after Him, we must know how He lived. To understand how He lived, we must study His life and know His Father.

## Map Your Journey

Think about your spiritual and mental consumption for a moment and open your heart to the Holy Spirit. As you read through the options for today, remember that condemnation (shame, guilt, etc.) is the sound of the enemy's voice, but conviction (remorse, sorrow, longing to change, etc.) is the timbre of the Holy Spirit.

### Journal Prompts

- How would you describe the health of your spirit-self?
- Prayerfully ask God if you are consuming anything that makes you spiritually unhealthy. Make a list (even if it's only one thing) and resolve to fast from it for a set period. Each day of your fast, journal about that particular thing: Why do you feel God asked you to give it up? What impact has it had on you? What changes do you see with it not being in your life, etc.?
- Make a list of things you believe about Jesus, and make another list of the things you know about God's character. Then, use a resource like BibleGateway.com or the YouVersion app to see if God's Word supports your beliefs. If you find something not supported by Scripture, cross it off!

### Deeper Study

- **Bread of Life**
  Deuteronomy 8:3; John 6:32–35; Luke 22:19
- **Spiritual Health**
  Ephesians 4:12–16; 1 Timothy 4:7–8; James 1:2–4; 3 John 1:2–4
- **Fasting**
  2 Corinthians 7:1; Galatians 5:16–26; Ephesians 4:20–24; Colossians 3:10

## Our Model

The Old Testament is full of prophecies about Jesus. God designed His covenant with Israel to point to the coming Messiah and our fully restored relationship with Him (John 5:39–40). In the midst of the prophesies, we catch glimpses of what Jesus would be like and how others would perceive Him. Read Isaiah 53:2–12; circle back to verse 2. How did He grow (a tender green shoot) amidst a dry and sterile ground (the world surrounding Him)? The New Testament offers one insight into how that might. Read Luke 2:39–52 and record what you learn about His childhood. What do we need to grow healthy in the unhealthy world surrounding us?

# Hear Him Speak

*"They won't follow a stranger; they will run from him because they don't know his voice."*

—John 10:5

God's Word is God-breathed, not man-made, and it is where we learn the sound of His voice. One of the hardest things for many people when they read the Bible is feeling the challenge of understanding it. Yet there are many translations available that can make this easier; finding one that works for you is key to successful Bible study. Remember feelings (being overwhelmed, intimidated, etc.) that keep you from His Word are not from the Lord. His voice draws us in; It doesn't push us away.

Just as there are many translations, there are many Bible reading plans. There is no right or wrong way to read the Bible, as long as your heart is open to the Holy Spirit. Sometimes it isn't the Bible itself that overwhelms us; it's the options. Instead of letting the possibilities intimidate us, we must shift our perspective. When one thing isn't working well, we must try something new. Options are solutions, not obstacles. This realization can help us turn a corner.

Regardless of where you are on your faith journey, I recommend first trying the New Living Translation. Various scholars from different Christian denominations translated from the original texts (the Hebrew Bible, Dead Sea Scrolls, Septuagint, Greek manuscripts, Samaritan Pentateuch, Greek New Testament, Testamentum Graece, and other manuscripts). This particular version is known as a thought-for-thought translation. Instead of translating each word separately, this

~ HEAR HIM SPEAK ~

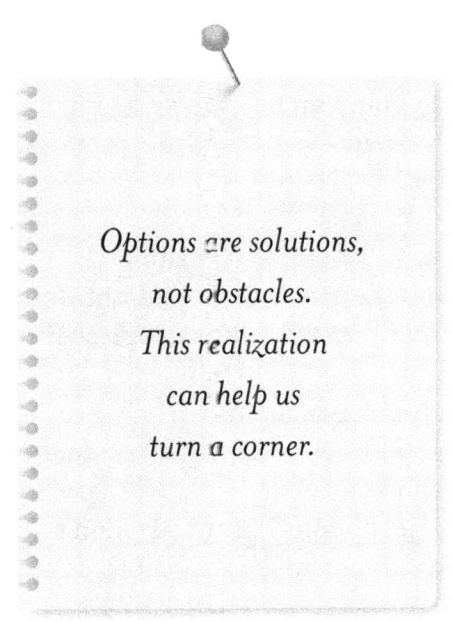

*Options are solutions, not obstacles. This realization can help us turn a corner.*

translation conveys the thoughts behind the text when a literal translation may be difficult to understand. One of the best features is that it uses modern-day equivalents to make it easier to understand rather than using ancient weights, measures, currency, and calendars which may be unfamiliar. (Don't worry about losing the original meaning; the word-for-word verbiage is available in the textual footnotes!)

When choosing a Bible reading plan, here are a few ideas to consider based on how often you currently read Scripture.

**Brand New**—If you have never really read the Bible before, start with one chapter a day. One of the Gospels (Matthew, Mark, Luke, or John) is a great place to start, but start in the New Testament regardless of where you begin. Trust me on this—the New Testament is where we learn about Jesus' life and sacrifice!

**Sporadic**—If you read the Bible sporadically and are looking to create a more intentional and consistent time with God, start with your favorite book of the Bible. If you don't have a favorite book, think of your favorite verse, and begin with that book. There are many Bible reading plans available online or through mobile apps. Ask your friends for recommendations. Just pick something that interests you!

**Faithful**—If you spend time daily in the Word already, continue with whatever Bible plan you are using. If it's not challenging you, and you're looking for something different to try, I recommend the SOAP (Scripture, Observation, Application, and Prayer) reading guide or a chronological reading plan; both are available online.

Another way to build a game plan can be as easy as knowing what kind of books you like to read. Your reading preference can guide you on where to start.

- Fiction—the Message translation, audio Bible
- Nonfiction—the Epistles, the Prophets, the Pentateuch
- Biographies—Gospels, Pentateuch, Chronological Bible, Historical books
- Poetry—Psalms, Proverbs, Ecclesiastes
- Short Stories—Gospels, Old Testament Bible "stories"
- Magazines—Epistles, shorter books
- None of the above (some people genuinely don't like reading or are auditory learners)—Audio Bible

Now that you know what you're going to read, how do you learn to hear God speak to you through your reading? The SOAP method of Bible study is an excellent option if you've never read with intentionality or if you struggle to hear His Voice when you read.

The great thing about this method is its simplicity. You don't have to write a novel (although you can); you can write one or two sentences and still get the benefit. It is essential to find what helps you most. If your Bible reading time becomes more of a task than an adventure, try a different reading plan or get ideas from other believers on what works for them—just don't give up.

**Scripture**—This is where you write the verse, verses, sentence, or key words you feel God is speaking to you.

- Before you start, say a short prayer asking the Holy Spirit to open your eyes and heart to show you what He wants you to reflect on today.
- Read the chosen passage, and as you do, highlight anything that pops out to you. Don't overthink it or

worry about why; just mark it. It may be a lot or a little—either is okay!
- After reading the entire passage, go back to the areas you highlighted and ask yourself, "Why did that stand out to me?" Focus on the one that prompts the most questions or thoughts for your journal entry.
- Start a new page in your faith journal and write the verse(s) or words at the top along with the reference (e.g., John 1:1).

**Observation**—This is where you start to figure out why the Holy Spirit led you to a particular verse or passage.

- In a sentence or two, write out why this passage caught your attention. Again, don't overthink it; simply write whatever comes to mind when you ask, "Why did that stand out to me?" It may even be questions you have about the text.

**Application**—This is the part that makes it life changing!

- Reread the verse and what you wrote, then ask, "What does that mean for me?"
- Write out what you think the Holy Spirit is showing you. It may be something He is encouraging you with, teaching you, or even asking you to change or grow stronger in. Perhaps it's something He wants you to study more deeply.

**Prayer**—This is where we let Him work!

- Write out a short prayer specifically focusing on the Application you just completed.

# Map Your Journey

No matter how well you know the Bible, God's Word is alive, and there is something new and fresh He wants to show you each day. Go into today's prompts with expectancy!

## Journal Prompts

- In what ways do you struggle with reading the Bible? What practical steps can you try to make it easier to hear what the Spirit is saying to you?
- Would you consider your Bible reading brand new, sporadic, or faithful? What is one small step you can take to improve the impact of His Word in your life?
- Choose a passage or verse and complete your first SOAP journal entry.

## Deeper Study

- **Holy Spirit**
  John 14:17, 16:13–15; 1 Corinthians 2:13–15
- **Understanding**
  Psalm 119:18; Acts 8:30–35; 2 Timothy 2:7; 2 Thessalonians 2:15
- **Implementation**
  Psalm 119:105; Philippians 4:9; James 1:22, 2:14–26

## *Our Model*

The Father spoke to Jesus most notably after His baptism, but God also spoke in two other recorded instances during Jesus' ministry on earth. Read Matthew 3:13–17, Matthew 17:1–9, and John 12:23–30. As you read these passages, reflect on three things:

1. What did God say?
2. Who heard Him speak?
3. How did people respond to His voice?

God speaks to each of us through His Word, His Spirit, other believers, our circumstances, and even His creation, but we may not always recognize His voice, or we may be confused by it. After reading these instances, what is the Spirit teaching you about His Voice and how you should respond to Him?

Make a note in your journal of a time when you know God spoke to you; include what He said and how you responded. Did He provide anyone to confirm that it was Him speaking? (This could have been a pastor who preached a message on a verse you read the day before, a friend who sent an encouraging text confirming what the Spirit prompted during your prayer time, or even a song that came on the radio affirming His love for you when you needed it most.) God often sends confirmations so we don't feel confused or conflicted. It reassures us that we are learning His voice. He gives us His peace so we can know that we are walking in the truth of His Word to us.

# Learn Truth

*"Anyone who belongs to God listens gladly to the words of God. But you don't listen because you don't belong to God."*
—John 8:47

Does a lot of noise easily overstimulate you? I know it does me! We live in a noisy world, and it seems never-ending at times. I love it when I'm able to go up in the mountains or out to a campsite for a few days and listen to the silence. The noise level in that environment isn't taxing. It isn't full of endless questions or relentless demands. It's so quiet that I can hear things I don't often hear in my everyday life—leaves rustling, water trickling, even the gentle breeze. God's Word is that place for us on our faith journeys. Why? Because it silences the noise. It quiets the voices that compete for our attention.

Why don't we go there more often if that's the case? Why don't we escape to God's mountain when the noise overwhelms us? Because that same noise holds us captive. The enemy uses the voices around us to distract us and lead us away from the gently spoken words of our Lord.

One of the most common things we hear people say in a controversial discussion is, "Well, I believe..." There are many different beliefs and many opinions that claim to be correct. Some people claim that "right" is an illusion, while others profess that "right for you" is what matters. But these are fallacies concocted by a deceiver to make us feel better about ourselves and to push God out of the picture. They create a god-like view of ourselves and distort His actual truth. If it worked in the Garden...

We must realize that what we believe is not nearly as

important as what God believes. He is the Creator of all. He is all-knowing. He is holy. Without Him we cannot differentiate truth from lies; His Word guides us into Truth. When we recognize our need for an absolute Truth—one that can be trusted and does not change—that is when our hearts genuinely open to Scripture, and our root systems begin to expand.

Many people claim that some of the Bible is accurate or historically relevant, but those beliefs leave us uncertain about whether or not we can trust His Word. If we do not believe that the Bible is without error and written through God's divine inspiration, then we will struggle to determine which parts are trustworthy and which parts are not. Without belief in an absolute Truth, we have no plumb line. Without accepting that God knows more than we do, we follow a fluid truth. We are limited in our understanding—He is not. Putting faith in God's Truth may mean letting go of our own. If this is you, can I lovingly challenge you for a moment? Psalm 34:8 boldly invites us to "taste and see that the Lord is good." He wants us to bring our questions to Him; He wants to give us clarity.

One of my youth leaders helped me to understand Scripture's inerrancy this way: first, he asked me, "Do you believe God is all-powerful and wants us to know His love for us?" I nodded. "Then think of it this way: God wrote His children a love letter, the Bible, to make sure that we would know of His limitless love for us and to ensure we had the information we need to find salvation and live the best life possible on this earth. While it's feasible man messed it up along the way, do you truly believe that an all-powerful God would allow that to happen? Would a loving, omnipotent Father allow the distortion of His love letter to us? Would He leave us floundering, unsure of the Truth, and with no basis to view the world?" No! I don't believe He would.

If you struggle with the idea of supernatural inspiration or the inerrancy of the Bible, then I invite you to submit that belief to the Lord in prayer. Taste the goodness of Scripture and see that He is good, and His Word is, too.

## Map Your Journey

This topic challenges us because it reveals our pride. Before reading through today's prompts, decide if you are ready to set aside your own beliefs to pursue His. Confess that decision in prayer, then select at least one Journal Prompt and one Deeper Study section below.

### *Journal Prompts*

- If you don't believe His Word is inerrant and inspired, make a list of your reasons. For a few minutes, prayerfully reflect on what you have written. Do your reasons give more credit to human wisdom or to God's Sovereignty and Omnipotence?
- What ideas or beliefs do you have about the world that you have never compared to God's Word? Would you be willing to lay those aside if you found that Scripture spoke contrary to your personal beliefs? Why or why not?
- Consider a time when your desires or ideas contradicted the Bible. Write about how God used that to deepen your faith.

### *Deeper Study*

- **His Inspired Word**
  Deuteronomy 18:18; Jeremiah 1:9; 2 Peter 1:16–21
- **Trustworthiness of His Word**
  Proverbs 30:5–6; Isaiah 55:8–11; John 1:1, 17:17; Hebrews 6:18–19
- **His Word Endures**
  Psalm 119:160; Isaiah 40:8; Matthew 5:18; 1 Peter 1:23–25

## *Our Model*

Start by reading John 1:1. We must understand that Jesus was and is the Word. There is nothing more reliable or trustworthy than Christ. He is the physical embodiment of God's Word to us and for us. Because of this, we can use Jesus and Scripture to help us understand the trustworthiness of the Bible.

Read John 5:31–32 and John 8:12–14, 42–47. In the first passage, Jesus states that self-witness is insufficient. Later, in chapter 8, when Jesus claims to be the light of the world (vs. 12), the Pharisees attempt to correct Him by stating that His testimony is not valid (vs. 13). In defense, the Lord explains that because He is the Son of God, self-witness is, in fact, reliable (vs. 14). Self-witness is reliable only when sin does not interfere. Because Jesus is God and therefore guiltless, we can trust His words. Similarly, since the Bible is God's Word, we can trust its claims. It is the enemy, and our prideful arrogance, that we should not trust.

What is God speaking to your heart today about His trustworthiness? What is He saying about the reliability of His Word? What step of faith is He asking you to take to trust Him fully?

# Apply and Grow

*But don't just listen to God's word. You must do what it says. Otherwise, you are only fooling yourselves.*

—JAMES 1:22

Applying Scripture to our daily lives may feel overwhelming depending on how you were raised (or not raised) in faith. If you were taught that only biblical scholars could interpret Scripture, you may feel unqualified and might be afraid to try. If you weren't exposed to God's Word growing up, the sheer size of the Bible might intimidate you and leave you feeling inadequate. Even if you were taught the importance of God's Word from a young age, you risk misapplication if you are too comfortable. No matter where you are right now, applying what you read brings growth.

If you have a table full of the healthiest, choicest foods, and you smell them and comment on their perfection but do not partake of them, they do no good to your physical body. You must consume them and digest them for their benefits to have any impact. We consume God's Word when we read it; we digest it when we apply it to our lives.

How do we learn to apply it and not take it out of context, especially if we don't have a seminary degree or lead a megachurch? It's not as hard as you think; in fact, we've been talking about it throughout the last few chapters.

- **Learn the voice of the Holy Spirit.** Trust Him and what He says. Remember, God's Word is living and active; He speaks to us through it; we must be ready to

listen, receive, and be willing to be fertilized and pruned. Fertilization comes in the form of encouragement and hope. Pruning is the process of removing the dead leaves and buds that stunt our growth.
- **Be willing to study, not just read.** There are so many great resources and methods for Bible study. SOAP is a good starting point, but techniques like verse mapping and book/character studies help us dive deeper when we want a more comprehensive understanding. These tools allow us to see areas of His character and ourselves that we would never find by merely skimming the surface. A simple online search can be valuable in providing various books that help you unpack Scripture.
- **Surround yourself with Spirit-led believers** and seek prayer and counsel when you are confused or unsure. We aren't meant to walk our faith journeys alone. It is the same narrow path that all believers travel, and we can use the wisdom and experience of others to help navigate our way to finding clarity in Scripture.

Misunderstanding passages or looking at verses out of context is one way the enemy tries to deceive us, but we don't have to fall victim to his plan. Start with a study Bible. Most study Bibles have a section for each book that provides helpful introductory information like who wrote the book, when and why it was written, and even the setting and cultural norms of the time. Read these!

It is also important not to simply read a single verse and use that as a foundation for your belief system. Always read the verses before and after, preferably the whole section or chapter, to see the entire situation surrounding the verse itself. Don't be lazy with your study; take the time to understand the context. A daily devotional helps us fix our thoughts on God, but it does not take the place of Bible study. Don't rely solely on the "verse a day keeps the devil away" approach. Strategically plan study time into your week and strengthen this discipline as often as possible.

## Map Your Journey

We have to read to hear, and we have to study to apply what we read correctly. Think about the current effort you're putting into studying God's Word and, if you haven't before, complete at least one Deeper Study.

## Journal Prompts

- Is studying something you enjoy, or does it trigger a negative emotional response? Take a few minutes today to walk through those feelings—good or bad—and ask the Holy Spirit to create a hunger in you for His Word.
- Choose one of the Deeper Study prompts below and do a SOAP journal for each verse listed. Go over each entry and summarize what the Spirit is asking you to apply.
- Think about how often you study (not just read) the Bible. Select a topic that interests you and dive into it over the next few days. Be sure to chronicle what you're learning in your faith journal!

## Deeper Study

- **Application**
  Matthew 7:24–25; Romans 2:13; James 1:22–25
- **False Teachers**
  Matthew 7:15–22; Acts 17:11;
  2 Corinthians 11:2–4, 13–15;
  2 Timothy 4:3–4; 1 John 4:1
- **Studying**
  Joshua 1:8; Ezra 7:10; Psalm 119:15–16, 97–98

## *Our Model*

We learn in 1 John 2:6 that we are to live our lives as Jesus did. As we've been walking this journey together, we have learned that Jesus prioritized time with His Father (Part 2: Gratitude) and that He knew Scripture (Part 3: Healthy Digestion). Many of the words of Jesus we read in the New Testament were quotations or paraphrases of the written Law—what we now refer to as the Old Testament. Much like today, the Jewish religion at that time took God's Word and developed its own traditions and perspectives. When you read, "You have heard it said..." Jesus isn't necessarily quoting directly from Scripture; He sometimes references the religious interpretations of His day.

Read through Matthew 5:21–42 and Matthew 15:1–20, and as you do, challenge yourself with the following action plan:

- Use the Bible footnotes to locate the original verses.
- Consider the original passage for yourself.
- Reflect on how Jesus' explanation shifted the cultural perspective.

Like some churches today, the Pharisees harmonized the teachings of the written Scripture with their own beliefs. Many considered their interpretation progressive because they aligned it with their own ideas. That is not the type of application that leads to spiritual growth; it is the type that leads to man-made religion. Read how Jesus addresses this approach to Scripture in John 5:39–40. Prayerfully ask the Holy Spirit if there are areas where you have used Scripture to support your own beliefs rather than basing your belief system on Christ.

# Memorize and Fight

*I have hidden your word in my heart that I might not sin against you.*

—Psalm 119:11

Okay, I'm keeping it real; memorizing Scripture is hard for me. I don't have the best memory. I'm a storyteller, not a dates and places kind of girl. When I say hard, I mean it requires a lot of effort, practice, and review to retain God's Word in my brain. Because of this, I didn't memorize Scripture for a very long time. But here's what God has shown me in the past few years—He created me, so He knows me. He does not expect me (or you) to do anything exactly the same way as anyone else because He made each of us unique. Instead of wanting what others have (memories that work), I have learned to be content with how He designed me. Don't get me wrong; I still ask Him to heal my memory issues! In the meantime, I have struggled to find a way to memorize Scripture that works for me. If you have a great memory, a photographic memory, or if you are part of that fantastic group with an eidetic memory, you probably need to prioritize memorizing His Word, and the rest will fall into place.

For everyone else…are you familiar with the phrase, "something is better than nothing?" (Hint: I've used it before!) Well, we're going to start there. If you were to memorize one verse a year, would it be more than you did last year? Start there. For some of you, it may be one a month; for others, it may be one a week, and for those super gifted people from the last paragraph, it may be one a day or one hour. No matter! Memorizing His

## ~ Memorize and Fight ~

Word helps us stockpile nourishment for when we are under siege.

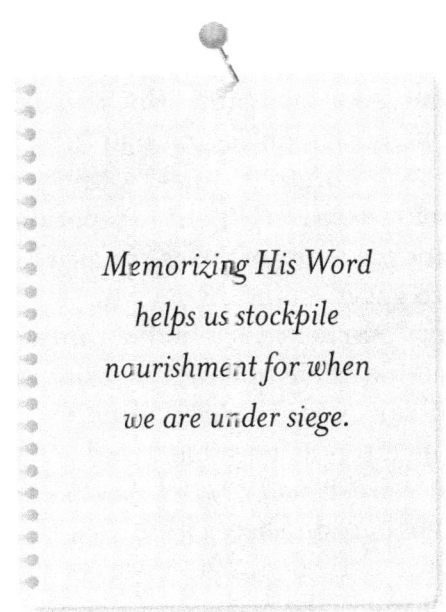

*Memorizing His Word helps us stockpile nourishment for when we are under siege.*

There are times when life is hard, a circumstance arises, or the enemy launches a blindside attack—and it is not usually during your quiet time with Jesus. Those memorized verses are the reserves in our spiritual pantries that we can count on when the enemy shows up unexpectedly. The human body stores fat so that when we are experiencing a lack of food, our bodies have fuel to use. Memorized Scripture creates a nutritional reserve for us spiritually.

Let me be clear—I grew up in Sunday school, and we had a weekly or monthly memory verse. I was on a Bible Quiz team in high school which required us to memorize entire chapters and books of Scripture. (I wasn't very good at it.) There are times, to this day, that those verses I fought to learn pop into my head exactly when I need them. I don't remember them perfectly, and I may not be able to tell you where in the Bible they are found, although sometimes, I do get the book right! But remember, those book titles, chapter references, and tiny little verse numbers are an organizational system added by man to reference God's Holy Word. When I realized that the words in the Bible were the valuable part, a weight fell off of my shoulders. And let's be honest, when we need to know where to find a passage, we can quickly look it up using the internet or a smartphone. If you're like me, stop expecting yourself to memorize perfectly and just start to memorize.

I'm going to share some tips and ideas to help you get

started, but before that, you need to select a verse! Your faith journal will come in handy here.

**Write it out**—Do you remember the *Little House on the Prairie* episodes when a student got in trouble and had to write "I will not..." on the chalkboard a hundred times? I know we don't see that much nowadays, but there is a benefit to repetition. Don't just write it once; write it once a day or three times a day, however many times it takes to get it rooted in your heart.

**Repeat after me**—Auditory learners need audio; that's all there is to it. Listen to it through a Bible app or a website and repeat it after the reader. You can record yourself and do the same thing—just verbalize it as often as possible.

**Post it everywhere**—Get a fresh pad of sticky notes and get to work! Write your verse on a dozen sheets and stick them everywhere—the mirror in your bathroom, the visor in your car, the monitor on your desk at work, the refrigerator door, the remote for your tv; get creative! Make sure you read it aloud, if you can, whenever you see it.

**Paper in the pocket**—Simple and easy—when you get up in the morning, write the verse on a piece of paper and slip it into your pocket. (I recommend the one where you keep your cell phone.) Every time you reach in your pocket and feel the paper, pull it out and read it. Every day rewrite a new piece of paper so you don't forget it in yesterday's pants.

**Make it into a song**—Music is not for everyone, but those artistic types tend to do well with this one. I still remember two verses from my Bible Quiz days that our youth pastor's wife made into a song. Many of our praise and worship songs are inspired by or include Scripture. There may already be a song with your verse in it—be sure to check.

**Break it into pieces**—Write it on an index card, then cover it to show only one line. When you've mastered that line, expose another line and practice the two together. You could even break the verse into pieces by writing a different phrase of words on each card; then practice putting them in order by scrambling and unscrambling the cards.

**Wallpaper/screensaver**—Pretty straightforward with this one. Find an image online with the verse or create one yourself and save it as the wallpaper on your phone or make it the screensaver for your computer or tablet.

**Rewrite it and make it personal**—When something is personal, it's easier to remember. There are a few ways you can do this:

- Insert your name in certain places.
  **Example:** "For I know the plans I have for [Michaela]," declares the Lord, "plans to prosper [her] and not to harm [her], plans to give [her] hope and a future." (Jeremiah 29:11)
- Convert it to a prayer you pray.
  **Example:** Lord, you are my light and my salvation—whom shall I fear? You, Lord, are the stronghold of my life—of whom shall I be afraid? (Psalm 27:1)

**Use an app**—I am sure there are many options out there, so look around. I recommend "Verses – Bible Memory" (by Verses Ltd. Co.; getverses.com) because I love it. There are a variety of translations available, and this mobile app uses games to help learn Scripture. Activities like "Reorder," "Fill in the Blank," and "Type It Out" are all designed for continual practice. This app also has tracking features that remind you to go back and review verses you've already learned and keep a record of your streaks. (Super helpful for competitively motivated people!)

Which method(s) stood out to you? Highlight it. Which one sounded like it might be fun? Highlight that one, too. Are there any ideas that have worked for you before? Yep, highlight those! Start with the highlighted items to help you commit a verse to memory. If you find it's not working, don't quit! Try another option. If none of these ideas suit your learning style, search online. Someone has figured it out somewhere and has posted something that can help. Remember, developing discipline means not giving up!

## Map Your Journey

The Bible is a big book, and memorization can feel intimidating if we listen to the enemy. Think about obstacles you've faced in the past or the ones consuming your thoughts right now, and surrender each one to the Lord before moving to today's prompts.

### Journal Prompts

- What is your favorite Bible verse? Write it out using at least three different translations.
- Select one verse from your faith journal and personalize it or transform it into a prayer. Then, read it every day for the next week.
- Review the ideas for memorization from this chapter and select one to try for at least one week.

### Deeper Study

- **Spiritual Battle**
  2 Corinthians 10:3–5; Ephesians 6:10–18; Hebrews 4:12; 1 Peter 5:8–9
- **Protection**
  Psalms 18:30, 27:1; Proverbs 1:33; Isaiah 26:3–4
- **Memorize**
  Deuteronomy 6:6–9; Psalm 1:2–3; John 15:7–9

## Our Model

We don't often think about Jesus fighting spiritual battles because He was always victorious, yet He did multiple times during His ministry. He was fully human and wrestled with the desires of the flesh, just as we do (Hebrews 4:15). Being fully God allowed Him to resist those temptations and remain sinless, but His struggles also provide practical examples for us to experience victory. Read the following passages and note what human struggle He faced and His strategies to battle it.

- Luke 4:1–13
- John 6:66–69
- Matthew 27:11–14
- Luke 23:32–43

Read Ephesians 6:10–18 and develop a battle plan for yourself when temptation comes and your flesh fights for dominance.

# Part 4

## Community

*"You need to be in fellowship...*
*If you separate a live coal from the others, it will soon die out."*
—Billy Graham

# The Forest

*Two people are better off than one, for they can help each other succeed. If one person falls, the other can reach out and help. But someone who falls alone is in real trouble.*
—ECCLESIASTES 4:9–10

Do you remember the Parable of the Sower? Some seeds landed on soil covered in weeds (thorns) that choked the life out of them. Our close companions significantly impact whether we grow, and our environments directly affect our maturation. Unfortunately, we don't always see our surroundings clearly. Beautiful flowers may form a ring around us, but those buds may be weeds. Or it may seem we are planted in a barren wasteland, but there is a community of new growth about to spring forth.

Some of you may be wondering how on earth community is a discipline. Because it takes work and commitment. It is not easy. We often hear this idea relating to marriage, but it applies to all of our relationships. To understand how this discipline works, we need to put aside our preconceived notions, past experiences, and expectations. We need to look at His Word to find His picture of Christian community and to understand why we need it.

Several factors play a role in how we each view the concept of community: our gender, whether we are introverts or extroverts, believers or nonbelievers, all play a part. Let's be honest…life would be easy if it weren't for people! Just like most things in this world, relationships have pros and cons. In fact, it's the criteria we often use, a "good" relationship has more pros than cons, and a "bad" one weighs heavier on the negative side of the scale. We use the same type of scale to determine "toxicity," too. We know that toxic means poisonous, and the reality is that every relationship has some level of toxicity to it. We are all sinful, and sin is a poison that destroys. If you cut out the "toxic" relationships, you will end up alone.

The part I think we forget is that God knows this. More than that, He understands it. Jesus lived life among us; He had "good" and "bad" relationships. People hurt Him, used Him, betrayed Him, and let Him down. He gets it. That is why He left us explicit instructions on making the most of our time with each other. We have a blueprint for relationships and don't need to struggle to figure it all out. When we acknowledge Him as the architect, we understand that He has already done the hard part; we must simply follow His plans.

As an introvert you might say there is a tiny level of truth in the statement, "I don't need anyone; I'd be fine on my own." Maybe friends and family members have repeatedly let you down, so that rings true for you as well. I don't know your story, but I do know that the enemy presents isolation from each other as a good thing—a false truth. It looks good and sounds good, but God's Word tells us we grow in community. Both cannot be true.

I have lived in Florida for over twenty years, but I grew up in the Pacific Northwest, where trees and forests are the scenery no matter where you look. Florida is different. Palm trees are different. They are beautiful in their way, but they generally live apart from each other. Experts even recommend planting some types of palm trees at least twenty-feet apart! Interestingly, palm trees do not have a taproot. Their root system is relatively shallow compared to the trees where I'm from; their roots generally only grow in the top thirty-six inches of topsoil, where water and nutrients are plentiful.

Satan wants us to be palm trees: pretty, tall, decorative, and isolated with shallow roots. Why? Because life is full of storms. During my time in Florida, my family has gone through three major hurricanes that impacted the areas where we lived. I have learned that no matter how tall or impressive a palm tree is, a three-foot-deep root system doesn't do much when hurricane-force winds come through. Some fall. Some stand. Some fall and take others with them.

God has a different idea for us, though. Have you ever had the opportunity to lay on your back in a forest and look up at a canopy of trees with branches so intertwined it's like a maze trying to figure out which limb belongs to which tree? There is beauty in the chaos as the sun shines through the breaks in the leaves. And yet, there is also protection from the rain when the storm blows through. It's not perfect protection, but the kind that keeps the wind at bay and breaks the heaviness of the drops as they fall. What's impressive is that if you could see underground, you'd see much the same in their root structure. Not only deeper, but wider. It can be nearly impossible to tell which root goes to which tree; it's like a collection of hopelessly tangled necklaces.

Of course, we don't get hurricanes in Seattle. However, we get horrible wind and ice storms, and sometimes, trees do fall. One of the most unbelievable sights walking through the woods is seeing a fallen tree that isn't on the ground. The trees around it broke its fall, and the interwoven roots allowed the tree to remain planted. Yes, you are picturing it clearly; there are fallen trees still alive and growing, supported by the trees around them! I believe this is God's purpose in the discipline of community.

## Map Your Journey

Over our lifetimes we all develop unhealthy coping mechanisms. We build walls to protect our hearts from pain and, in doing so, create barriers in our relationships with God, too. The desire and need to protect ourselves is where the very problem lies. So, the first thing we're going to unpack for this discipline is self-awareness: understanding the health of our relationships.

### Journal Prompts

- How do you currently evaluate your relationships? Do you use a toxicity meter, a pros and cons list, or other criteria to determine relationship health? How does your process align with God's idea for relationships?
- Do you view yourself as a palm tree, or are you deeply rooted in a forest environment? Would you say that your friendships are primarily shallow or that your spiritual roots are intertwined? What steps might you take to deepen your roots and support system this week?
- When storms come, do you feel alone and isolated or supported by those around you? If you have people around you but don't feel supported, why do you think that might be? How can you work to strengthen those relationships to better model a biblical community?

### Deeper Study

- **Healthy Community**
  Acts 4:32–35; Romans 12:9–16; James 5:16
- **Strength in Storms**
  Exodus 17:8–13; 1 Corinthians 12:14–27; Galatians 6:2
- **Unity in the Church**
  2 Corinthians 13:11; Galatians 3:28; Colossians 3:14

## Our Model

Jesus deeply interwove His life with others. He had His multitude of followers, His twelve disciples, the three closest to Him, and the one He dearly loved. Jesus' relationships model healthy balance. Read the following passages and take notes. List anything you see Him doing to foster closeness with others (look for things like encouragement, intimacy, support, instruction, etc.).

- Matthew 4:21–22
- Matthew 13:10–17
- Matthew 15:29–39
- Matthew 20:17–19
- Mark 1:29–31
- John 21:1–13

Prayerfully ask Him to reveal one relationship that needs attention and ask Him to lead you in following His example.

# Worship

*All the believers devoted themselves to the apostles' teaching, and to fellowship, and to sharing in meals (including the Lord's Supper), and to prayer.*

—ACTS 2:42

The New Testament Church established some pretty great guidelines for us of what community in faith should look like, yet many churches today focus on one aspect over the others. Worshiping God is at the heart of everything He created us to do. Despite what many of us believe, community is not about how we can benefit from others; it's not even about how we can bless others. Community is about honoring God with our obedience. When we begin to see our relationships as an extension of our worship, as another way to adore God, we find spiritual health and community.

Let's take a closer look at this verse from Acts.

**Apostles' teaching**—the instructional aspect of the Church. It's sermons and Bible studies, marriage groups and mentorships. When we rely solely on our own understanding of Scripture, we miss the benefit of learning from God's work in others. We limit our capacity for growth when we only learn from ourselves. It's prideful to think we have nothing to gain from others, and it's wise to choose to learn from others' experiences and avoid pitfalls.

**Fellowship**—if you've been part of a church for very long, you may believe that the word "fellowship" means food and fun, but that's not really what biblical fellowship is. The Greek word *koinonia* means community, communion, joint participation, sharing, and intimacy, all of which are deeper than what I've found at the potlucks I've been to! Fellowship isn't about food at all. (In fact, that's the next thing we'll talk about!) Rather, fellowship is about connection. Yes, that can happen around a dinner table, but it happens more in our daily living: when we have a terrible day...when we find out we got the job...when a marriage is struggling...when a health diagnosis changes everything. Fellowship happens when we live life together. Jesus' disciples walked with Him daily for three years.

**Sharing meals**—potlucks and barbecues are important. When we join together around food, we have an opportunity to give thanks and to connect on a comfortable and easy level. Sharing communion and remembering what Christ did for us creates a truly blessed intimacy. In addition, sharing our resources by making a meal or treating a new family to lunch after church adds value to one another. Shifting our focus from ourselves and our needs to blessing others opens the door to authentic relationships, and food is an easy place to start!

**Prayer**—we've talked a lot about prayer in this book, but most of the focus has been on our own personal prayers. These believers devoted themselves to prayer, both personally and corporately, for their needs and the needs of others. They interceded together on behalf of other believers, Christ's Church, and the lost. In the same way that our personal prayer times are critical to growth, corporate prayer is crucial in building community. These opportunities occur in special prayer services, at the altar on Sunday mornings, or in small group studies. Let me encourage you never to miss a chance to pray with other believers.

If we keep reading in Acts 2, verse 43 tells us what happened as a result of their worshiping God through their relationships: "A deep sense of awe came over them all, and the apostles performed many miraculous signs and wonders." I think the deep sense of awe had a lot to do with the fact that this diverse and eclectic group of people were somehow all working and living together in peace and unity. That unity opened a gateway to heaven, and God poured out His Spirit, empowering the believers to demonstrate miraculous signs and wonders to the world. However, we must remember that the first miracle is the corporate worship experience found in the unique community He created for us.

*When we begin
to see our relationships
as an extension
of our worship,
as another way
to adore God,
we find spiritual health
and community.*

## Map Your Journey

If Christians or leaders in the Church have hurt you, the idea of community or connection may make you want to skip this chapter. I get that. I've been there. But here's the problem: when we cut ourselves off from God's community for any reason, valid or not, we reject His gift to us. We are choosing our way over His. It is a lot of work to be in a relationship with others, but it isn't just His recommendation; it's His plan. It isn't a command; it's a gift. The work is worth the reward—that's His promise to us.

### Journal Prompts

- Which of these areas (teaching, fellowship, sharing meals, prayer) are challenging for you? Why do you think that is? Submit it to the Lord in prayer, and then brainstorm a few ideas of what you can do this month to try and grow in that area.
- Are you feeling uncomfortable with this topic altogether? If so, take some time to think about why—not just on the surface, but dive deep. If you find a past hurt, go back to the chapter on repentance and take some time to work through it.
- Take some time to reflect on the idea of community as an expression of worship. Journal examples from your life when you've experienced a healthy Christian community.

*Deeper Study*

- **Teaching**
  Deuteronomy 32:2–4; Luke 6:39–40;
  Colossians 3:16–17; Titus 2:7–8
- **Fellowship**
  Matthew 18:20; Romans 1:12; Philippians 2:1–2
- **Resources**
  Acts 2:44–47; Romans 12:13; Hebrews 13:15–16;
  James 2:14–17
- **Prayer**
  Acts 4:31; Romans 12:12; 2 Corinthians 1:11;
  James 5:14–16

*Our Model*

We see Jesus celebrating various Jewish festivals and feasts throughout the Gospels, worshiping in fellowship. Matthew 26:17–46 provides a monumental example of community. As you read, look for the four areas (teaching, fellowship, sharing meals, and prayer) we discussed in this chapter. This passage is a heavy example of community, yet at the heart of it, we see Jesus modeling community worship. What can you learn from His example?

# Fellowship

*This is what the Lord says: "Stop at the crossroads and look around. Ask for the old, godly way, and walk in it. Travel its path, and you will find rest for your souls. But you reply, 'No, that's not the road we want!'"*

—JEREMIAH 6:16

When we walk on the right path—His path—it feels hard. It is not an easy road to travel, this path of righteousness. Jesus taught us in Matthew 7:13–14 that it wouldn't be: "You can enter God's Kingdom only through the narrow gate. The highway to hell is broad, and its gate is wide for the many who choose that way. But the gateway to life is very narrow, and the road is difficult, and only a few ever find it." Yet we are still surprised at the isolation we feel and the hazards we encounter. The darkness surrounding us and the length of the road can make us feel lost. I can't say it enough! God's plan is for us to live in community; the enemy's strategy to combat it is isolation.

So, let's talk about the road after the narrow gate and those four challenges we all face at some point.

**Isolation**—Jesus just said it in Matthew "...only a few ever find it." If only a few find the gate, it makes sense that the road isn't jam-packed with people. Finding people we enjoy spending time with who share our beliefs, values, and faith isn't always easy. They are there, but our faith journeys are unique, and we may not be at the same mile marker all time (if there were mile markers!), but the road is easier when you walk it with others. Walking a faith journey alone is possible, but progress

## FELLOWSHIP

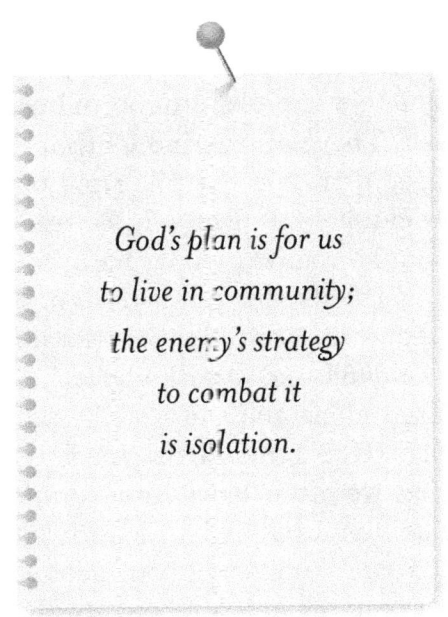

*God's plan is for us to live in community; the enemy's strategy to combat it is isolation.*

is slow, the obstacles often seem overwhelming, and discouragement lurks around every corner.

Fellowship is God's solution to the loneliness we can face on our faith walk. Many Christians say they don't need the Church or Christian friends, but that is a worldly mindset; it's not biblical. Not only did Jesus come to bring us eternal life, but He also came to experience humanity and model for us how God desires us to walk in relationship with Him. During His earthly ministry, Jesus had twelve close friends, and of those twelve, He had three best friends. If God's plan was for Jesus to walk His journey with others, wouldn't He expect us to do so as well?

**Hazards**—Yes, the path may have a pothole here and there or a fallen tree blocking the way. Those hazards are the obstacles we face living in a fallen world—broken relationships, unfair treatment, awful things like crime, the death of a loved one, and natural disasters; these can all feel overwhelming. Sometimes the challenges pile up one after another, and it feels like we are walking the worst-maintained road on the planet.

God's sovereignty is one of the hardest things to understand because we view love through a flawed lens. We think that loving parents protect their children from harm, but this is only partially true. Loving parents also teach their children how to survive pain when it comes. We must understand something essential: God knows about each obstacle we face before we ever get there. He strategically places them to help us learn to walk with Him. Character grows in hardship, so those hazards are by divine design. God desires to use those snags to cultivate a more intimate relationship with Him and with the people walking next to us. He gives us fellow travelers to remind us of the truth when we feel confused. They can remind us that the thorny bushes in the ditches keep us moving on the right path and in the right direction. They can help us over a fallen tree or help us move it off the path to make the way easier for others.

There are other hazards we face, also by divine design, but these are ones that we don't have to face; they are the ones we choose. They are the ones we don't like to talk about. They are the brambles He has planted along the sides of the path, and they are entirely avoidable. If we stay on the road, they have no impact whatsoever. Yet, we often have cuts, scrapes, and injuries because we change our minds when we find the way difficult. We return to our sins. We return to our past and resume mistakes we know have hurt us before. We want to go back to the wide, comfortable road where all our friends walk, the one we remember being so easy. Instead of listening to the wise counsel around us, we jump into the bushes, push through the thorns, and come out on the other side bleeding.

Forcing our way through these protective barriers causes unnecessary pain that God never intended for us to endure. Once we're on the other side and realize our mistake, it's hard for us to imagine a way to get back. The thorny vines suddenly seem as if He planted them there to keep us out. This flawed perspective is because our sins allow the enemy to deceive us. He twists the truth we know (those bushes are for our protection) and convinces us they are an obstruction God created to keep us away. When you find yourself here, don't believe it. Remember where you were and own the choices you've made. Ask Him to pick you up and return you to your rightful place on His path of righteousness. If you don't know how, find a fellow traveler and let them guide you back.

**Darkness**—The path of righteousness may not have streetlights every few feet, but what we do have as we walk is a lamp—a lamp to our path and a light to our feet—the guidance of His Word. Yet even this poses challenges. The first goes back to point #1. If we walk our faith journeys alone, our lamps only shine so brightly. If we invite and allow others to walk with us, we walk with accountability. His Word shines brightest when we all use it to light the path together.

The other thing we do is forget that we have a lamp. We look for other sources of light—the moon, the stars. Those lights may look like pastors, friends, social media, or news outlets. God never intended for one of those to be our guide. There is nothing wrong with sermons, podcasts, spiritual growth books, and so on, as long as we are seeking His voice above the input of others. If you find yourself reading or listening more to someone else telling you about the Bible than you do actually reading it, you may want to consider making an adjustment; perhaps you're using His lamp, but not at its full brightness. Be intentional in keeping God's Word the focus because the enemy will try to shift our center of attention to the people in our communities.

**Feeling Lost**—I wrestle the most with feeling lost. I am directionally challenged, and I use my GPS everywhere I go. I tell others it's because the app knows where the traffic is, but the whole truth is that it gives me confidence that I won't get lost. It is hard for me to walk a road when I don't know what is ahead. I struggle, and sometimes I just stop walking. Sometimes I feel so lost I sit in the middle of the road and cry. Here's what I'm learning, though: it's a straight road. It may not have mile markers to show precisely how far I've come or how much further I have to go. Without these markers, I can sometimes see things disproportionately. I can feel like I've barely moved and that I'll never reach my destination. But perception and perspective are not reality. The truth is that God knows every detail and every step. He has provided us with a path that doesn't have forks without guideposts. We never have to struggle with which way to choose as long as we keep moving forward. If we stay out of the brambles, the path is pretty clear. Take a step. Take another. This is faith in its purest form: we move, then He leads. We can also look to those around us to see that we are going the right way. Fellowship gives us affirmation that we are *not* lost.

## Map Your Journey

No matter how many steps you've taken so far, we all face these obstacles, and fellowship is key to overcoming them. Before beginning today's prompts, take a moment to reflect on your road so far. Many of us have been taught from a young age that if we are strong, we don't need others. Think about the relationship lessons you have learned along the way for a few minutes, and then select one or two action steps below.

### Journal Prompts

- Are you walking alone? Take a few minutes and ask God to show you the people He has placed beside you. They won't be perfect. You'll hurt and disappoint each other, but you'll also have a brighter light to walk by and someone to help with obstacles on the path. Make a list of expectations you've placed on others and prayerfully let them go.
- Are you tempted to change paths? Have you already started to move away from Him? If you feel stuck in the brambles, write out a prayer of repentance and ask for His help. He never wanted you to be where you are, and He's ready to place you back on His path. Reach out to a Christian friend or pastor; James 5:16 tells us to confess our sins to each other and pray for each other so that we may be healed.
- Does the idea of letting people get close terrify you? Stop and pray. Ask God to show you times in your life when He has provided others to help you. Make a list of every positive impact another person has had on your spiritual journey, then thank Him for each person He used to draw you closer to Him.

## Deeper Study

- **Walking Together**
  Proverbs 27:17; 2 Corinthians 3:20-24; Philemon 1:16-17; 1 John 1:3, 7
- **Support**
  2 Corinthians 1:7; Philippians 4:14-15; Hebrews 10:33; 1 Timothy 6:18
- **Encouragement**
  Romans 14:19; Galatians 2:9; Hebrews 10:23-25

## Our Model

We often consider Jesus' relationships with the disciples when we think about His fellowship with others. Yet, there are many other meaningful relationships Jesus had that can help us see how He allowed others to draw close. Mary, Martha, and Lazarus are beautiful examples of this. These siblings are mentioned multiple times in Scripture. Read Luke 10:38-42, John 11:1-43, and John 12:1-8 to peek into their relationships with our Lord. Take note of the relationship pitfalls (jealousy, sickness, grief, priorities, etc.) and reflect on how Jesus responded to each. Does this align with how you fellowship with others? Why or why not?

# Restored Relationships

*"I am the Lord, the God of all the peoples of the world. Is anything too hard for me?"*

—Jeremiah 32:27

Church families, like our biological families, are not perfect. Friends who are "like family" are not perfect. We live in a broken world full of broken people, so we must live in the reality of broken families—biological, church, and even friends. People deal with broken relationships in many different ways. After being hurt, some of us write the person off. It's the "You're Dead to Me" approach. Others blame themselves and carry the responsibility for every misstep in a "Proud to Be A Martyr" perspective. Some of us are the ones who do the hurting to avoid pain ourselves in a "Gotcha First" mindset. I'm sure there are many others, and sometimes we are a little bit of all of them. So if relationships will always cause pain because we are all broken, what's the point?

Let's take a look at why we have broken relationships. God first established the concept of relationship when He created Adam. It was a perfect relationship. Once Adam chose to sin, he broke the relationship he had with God. Unfortunately, that brokenness spilled over into our human relationships as well. Adam blamed Eve for his choices, and their children were born into a broken family. But God had a plan to heal our relationships with Him by sending His own Son, Jesus, to be the bridge to rebuild and restore our connection. That same bridge can also heal our relationships in the family of faith. If we look to God as our model, we can learn how broken relationships can be redeemed and restored.

The first thing that happened with our sin was that we hurt God. We need to recognize that being hurt is unavoidable. We don't like that answer, so some of us build walls around our hearts to protect ourselves from pain, yet we still get hurt. So we make the walls higher and let fewer people in, but still, the hurt happens. Others take the opposite approach. They let everyone in, hoping they will find the one or two people who won't let them down, but they don't. They start to think the problem is with them, that they are unlovable. If we look honestly at both scenarios, we realize that neither option actually works because people still hurt us. Why do we keep trying things that don't work? We cannot control whether we get hurt or not, but we can control how we handle the pain when it happens. What if we try something different? Let's look at how God responded to Adam and Eve after they hurt Him (Genesis 3:9–24):

- He looked for them. (verse 9)
- He gave them an opportunity to confess. (verse 11)
- He expressed His disappointment. (verse 13)
- He explained the consequences of their choices. (verses 14–19)
- He cared for them. (verse 21)
- He protected them. (verse 22–24)

He loved them and provided a way for the relationship to be healed (first by the laws and sacrifices, then through Jesus).

Despite everything God did for us, the choice of restoration remains up to us, the offenders. What if we were to take that same approach in our relationships, specifically in our relationships with other believers? We have family and friends who do not know the Lord, so they do not share our biblical worldview or our biblical approach to conflict. Because they remain disconnected from God, they are not likely to understand how to reconnect with others. But in the world of believers, it should look different. We should all be seeking to follow God's way in our relationships. When we do, miracles happen.

Yet, even as Christ followers, we all too often choose the world's view of relationships instead of God's. We say, "it's no big deal," and stuff the hurt inside, or we decide to talk to everyone but the person who hurt us about the issue. We may even end the relationship without attempting to work through it. Why? Because the enemy loves broken relationships. He loves it when the church looks just like the world. He twists and distorts our perspectives like a funhouse mirror. If he can keep us from talking about the issue, he can keep us believing whatever lies he's fed us. We continue to look in the relationship mirror and see a monstrosity distorted beyond repair. It's not true, and it is **not** how God intended for us to walk through life. In fact, Jesus repeatedly says in the Gospels that what sets His followers apart from the world is their love for one another and their unity. Is that what you see when you look at His Church? What about when you look at your life?

So, what do we do within Christian community? Let's go back to Genesis for the answer. First, we seek out the person who hurt us. Why? Because there is an excellent chance they never meant to hurt us and don't even know that they did. When we reach out to them, we acknowledge that the relationship is too important to write off. We must be honest and vulnerable when we reach out, which is often challenging because we are already hurt. Now we are exposing ourselves to potentially more pain or even rejection. But here is the truth, if you tell someone that what they did was hurtful, and you explain why and how it made you feel, you are allowing them to repent for a sin they may not even realize they committed. Too often, we assume the hurt was intentional when it wasn't. This conversation opens the door for both of you to mature in your faith. We learn to believe the best in others instead of the worst, and we often find healing when we think it's impossible. If they aren't receptive, well, that's between them and Jesus. You did your part (Romans 12:18).

Depending on the offense, there may be consequences for the offender. Broken trust must be rebuilt. When words cause wounds, there must be bandaging and healing. The purpose of consequences isn't about making someone do penance. Forgiveness is freely given to us by God and must be freely given to others by us. Consequences are about healing. What do you need (if anything) from that person in order to heal? It may be that you need to hear them say, "I am so sorry; I didn't realize I hurt you." If it's a repeated offense, it might require a little distance to let God heal you and continue His work in them. We know that we confess our sins to God for forgiveness, but His Word also teaches us that we find healing when we confess our sins to one another.

After those first hard steps, Scripture teaches us that God cared for Adam and Eve, and He protected them. That's right, He, the offended, cared for and protected the offender. This approach is definitely **not** something either the world or our human natures endorse. But you need to know that this doesn't mean they got away with it; we know that isn't true. It means He loved them more than their offensive behavior and was willing to do what was best *for them*. For us, that means we pray for them, and we don't go around telling everyone what they did. It means that we love them enough not to continue holding their mistakes against them, and we love God enough to follow His example of grace and mercy.

## Map Your Journey

I know this is a complicated topic. You may have experienced deep trauma or abuse, and it's imperative for you to hear this: I am so sorry. That was *not* God's plan for you, and it broke His heart, too. We must remember that He is our Great Physician, and He wants to heal those wounds and set you free from the pain they caused. Open your heart to the work He wants to do as you select your prompts for today.

### *Journal Prompts*

- What broken relationships within your church family might God want to heal? What is He asking you to do about it (pray for them, seek forgiveness, have a hard conversation, etc.)?
- Prayerfully ask God if there is someone you have hurt. Write about who and what happened. Allow the Holy Spirit to lead you if there is something He asks you to do to make it right.
- Write about a restored relationship. We need to remember the miracles God has done so we can boldly work on our relationships in the future.

### *Deeper Study*

- **Reconciliation**
  Genesis 50:19–21; Proverbs 17:9; Matthew 5:23–24; 2 Corinthians 5:18–19
- **Forgiveness**
  Matthew 6:12–15; Ephesians 4:32; Colossians 3:13; 1 John 2:9–11
- **Dealing with Conflict**
  Matthew 18:15–17; Luke 17:3; Romans 15:7; Hebrews 12:14–15

## Our Model

Stop and think about everything you know about what Jesus went through during His betrayal, arrest, trials, conviction, and crucifixion. Make a list of all the hurtful details you remember. When you finish, read Luke chapters 22–23; add to your list if you missed any specifics.

Look over your list and consider every emotional and physical wound He endured; perhaps you can relate to many of them. Now, circle back to Luke 23:34. There are two profound aspects to His statement in this verse we often hear quoted. First, He forgave them. That is a hard enough idea to grasp and an even harder example to follow. But what about the second part? "...they don't know what they are doing." You read the verses; clearly, they knew. Open your heart to the Holy Spirit and ask the Lord what He meant.

Forgiveness and believing the best in others isn't easy, but there is a reason God commands it, and Jesus modeled it. Who is the Lord asking you to forgive?

# Unity

*...Be joyful. Grow to maturity. Encourage each other. Live in harmony and peace. Then the God of love and peace will be with you.*

—2 Corinthians 13:11

Unity is a buzzword we hear quite a bit; yet, like many words, the world's definition and God's aren't always in alignment. Most people would agree that unity is a great goal, but if we don't recognize that the word means different things to different people, then we aren't moving in the same direction, are we? If we look to God's Word, our absolute and unwavering truth, then we, as believers, can begin to move toward the same goal.

To better understand the biblical idea of unity, let's talk about what unity is not. It is not equality. It is not tolerance. It is not uniformity. It *is* having a like-mind, a group of people moving in the same direction step-by-step. Picture a marching band. There are certain similarities in uniform and posture, but each member is still uniquely individual. Band members have their own instruments and parts to play yet still have their own unique God-given personalities. So, if we consider God's Church within those parameters, we can begin to see why it's good for us to be in unity.

The Church as a whole ought to be moving in the same direction and playing the same song. We all wear the uniform of Christ's righteousness and the same spiritual armor. We all stand proud, knowing we are His. This unity makes a marching band remarkable to hear and beautiful to watch. I'm not talking about keeping up appearances or conformity. When Christ is truly our Lord, we begin to look more like Him, not like one another.

Yet, as individuals, we are responsible for becoming skilled with our instruments and knowing our parts in the music. The Drum Major assigns our instruments. He knows our talents and areas that need improvement, so His assignment is always perfect. Learning our parts in the music is where unity gets complicated. Imagine if the tuba player started following the music for the French horn, or the snare drum switched music with the cymbals—there'd be a cacophony! Nothing about that music would spread joy or attract others.

The principal thing to remember about unity is that we are only responsible for our parts! Romans 12:18 puts it quite simply: "Do all that you can to live in peace with everyone." Practice the instrument assigned to you and focus on the music you are responsible for knowing. Anyone who isn't doing those things is the problem of the Drum Major, not us. He will adjust and correct each band member as He sees fit.

If we're going to do our part well, we must know what it is. On a fundamental level, we can look to this chapter's verse. Be joyful. Grow to maturity. Encourage others. Live in harmony. Focus on yourself, not anyone else. Musicians practice, and so should we. Give yourself little homework assignments each day or week.

On a deeper level, we must take the time to learn our instruments. Scripture gives us multiple lists of spiritual gifts, and there are a variety of spiritual gift assessments available online that can help you discover what instrument you play in God's marching band. Here are some examples: prophecy, serving, teaching, exhortation, giving, leadership, and mercy (Romans 12); word of wisdom, word of knowledge, faith, gifts of healing, miracles, distinguishing between spirits, tongues, and interpretation of tongues (1 Corinthians 12); speaking and helping others (1 Peter 4).

## Map Your Journey

Do you spend more time noticing the discord and wrong notes of other players, or are you singularly focused on your music so that you're able to identify where you need to improve? Before you dig deeper into today's journey, confess any critical spirit or judgment you've had toward others, and ask the Holy Spirit to help you focus on yourself today.

### Journal Prompts

- What instrument in the band of Christ has God assigned you to play? How would you rate your current skill level—novice, beginner, intermediate, or advanced? What are some ways you could practice and improve your skill?
- How has God uniquely created you for your specific part in the band? What natural talent do you have in this calling?
- Are you using your skills and gifts to make a joyful noise? When we sense God's peace and love, we know we are in harmony with His music.

### Deeper Study

- **Joy**
  Proverbs 17:22; Romans 14:17, 15:13; 1 Peter 1:8
- **Unity**
  John 13:35; Ephesians 4:2–3; Philippians 3:15–16
- **Spiritual Gifts**
  Romans 1:11, 11:29; Ephesians 4:11–12;
  2 Timothy 1:6–7

## *Our Model*

Sometimes unity in the Church feels impossible. We see firsthand the jealousy, self-promotion, false witness, and more. We know unity is essential, but it just doesn't seem realistic. Crucial teaching concerning Christian unity is from Jesus Himself in John 17:21. After you read it, take some time to prayerfully ponder the following questions:

- We know that perfection isn't possible, and unity sounds like a utopian ideal, but would Jesus ask His Father to do something that wasn't miraculously possible?
- We know Jesus and the Father are One; what would it look like for His Church to reflect that?
- Why is unity so important to Jesus?
- How can you shift your priorities to make it important to you as well?
- What role might you play in Jesus' prayer being answered?

# Discipleship

*Don't let anyone capture you with empty philosophies and high-sounding nonsense that come from human thinking and from the spiritual powers of this world, rather than from Christ.*
—COLOSSIANS 2:8

Left to ourselves, we are more easily led astray by the enemy's deceptions. It used to be easier to know God's truth because it was believed by the majority, at least in America. The shift in our culture to a post-Christian worldview has caused all levels of confusion for the Church. As Christ followers, there is so much more that we have to filter. But this isn't a bad thing. It is forcing us to mature. We can no longer rely on the word of others; we must seek God's Word on matters ourselves. This verse starts with the phrase "don't let..." which indicates a level of responsibility to the believer. We choose what we believe, and we decide whether we want to know if those beliefs align with His.

I'm not telling you that the connection to community is to ignore everyone else because they might be wrong. What I do want to help you understand is that discipleship is critical. This "church-y" word is often thrown around in Christian circles, yet not everyone knows or understands how it truly looks. We defined disciple back in Part 1, and discipleship takes it one step further. A disciple is a follower or student of a teacher, leader, or philosopher. So, in short, discipleship is the process we walk through in becoming a disciple. Discipleship is when you stop expecting others to do for you and begin looking for ways that you can do for others. It's the transformation from self-focused to others-focused, and it is a lifelong process.

If you recall, my purpose in writing this book is to share what the Holy Spirit has taught me in the hope that it will help you in your journey. I want to disciple you. And in turn, it is my prayer that you take what the Holy Spirit teaches you and disciple someone else. In all the years I spent in full-time ministry, lay ministry, and participating in church, God has been teaching me the path to discipleship.

**Step 1—Salvation: God does for you.** Our journeys begin with an act that only God can accomplish. His Spirit draws us close, and we accept His free gift of salvation. He created us in the womb, and He recreates us in Spirit.

**Step 2—Infancy: Others do for you.** Our rebirth begins like our physical birth; we are highly dependent on others to help us survive. We don't know very much about faith, God, or His Word when we begin. So we listen to sermons, read spiritual growth books, and buy devotionals. We need the insight and wisdom of those who've walked before us.

**Step 3—Growth: You learn to do for yourself.** As we get to know God for ourselves, we grow. We don't believe He's good because of what others say or what we read. We believe it because we've experienced it ourselves. Our relationships with Him shift to include our personal encounters with Him. The longer we walk with Him, the better we know Him. The more we are vulnerable before Him, the better we know ourselves.

**Step 4—Maturity: You do for others.** Many believers finish their lives without reaching full maturity. They never learn to say as Paul did, "Follow my example, as I follow the example of Christ" (1 Corinthians 11:1 NIV). We are called to be an example, share our testimonies of His goodness, and lead others along the path.

This growth process is where our journeys meet true biblical community, when we go from consuming to producing to distributing. Uniqueness is a beautiful aspect of all God's creation, including us. This road that leads from being discipled to discipling others is a remarkable path, but it is unique for each of us.

## Map Your Journey

The beauty of God's plan is that we learn to love as He loves; it is not for what we can get from others but for what we can give. Is that not what He's done for us? Settle your heart and think about all He has given you with no gain to Himself, and as your heart fills with gratitude, select your prompt for today.

### Journal Prompts

- When you look at where you are today in your faith journey, what step would you say you are on? How long have you been in this place? Do you think God might be calling you to something more?
- As our physical bodies mature, clear signs are visible to the world. What signs of spiritual maturity can you see in others? In yourself?
- Reflect on who has discipled you. What did they teach you? Why was it helpful for your growth? Now ask the Lord if there is someone He wants you to come alongside in a similar way.

### Deeper Study

- **Maturity**
  1 Corinthians 14:20; Ephesians 4:13–15; Hebrews 5:11–6:3
- **Discipling Others**
  Colossians 1:9–10, 28–29; 2 Timothy 2:2; Jude 1:3–4
- **Setting an Example**
  Matthew 5:16, 43–48; Ephesians 5:1–10; Philippians 3:17–18; Titus 2:6–7

### Our Model

Jesus, as He always has been, is the only perfect model. The sacrifice we most often reflect on is His surrender on the cross. Read the passages below and look for other ways that Jesus modeled putting the needs of others before His own.

- Mark 4:35–41
- Mark 6:30–44
- Luke 8:40–56
- John 2:1–12
- John 4:1–10

Ask the Holy Spirit to lead you today, to show you when you can set aside your needs for someone else's good.

# Acknowledgements

There are so many people who played a part in writing this book; I wish I could thank each of you by name. To anyone who has walked a step of this journey with me, thank you. There are certain people who I must acknowledge, because without them, this book would not be completed: my cheerleaders and prayer team, Carlotta Denney and Georgeann Lytle; those who were there as the vision started to unfold, Connie Nabor and Christina Rasmussen; my editing team, Jodi Aiken, Jennifer Breeze, Robin Connett, Melanie Erker, and Judi Van Cleave; my beta readers, Kelly Beversdorf and Dorina Charlton; my patient publishing team at WestBow Press, Eric Schroeder, Hanna Nate, Bob DeGroff, and all of the other amazing people who got this book to print. Of course, I would never have finished without the support of my husband, who pushed me and motivated me. (Thanks for the salted caramel Pizookies®!) But above all, my heavenly Father, who knew the plan for this book long before I did. It's all for Your glory.

> *May it one day be said of me: "I brought glory to you here on earth by completing the work you gave me to do." (John 17:4)*

# Author Bio

Michaela L. Carson is a biblically-guided author and speaker who has served in Christian ministry for over 25 years. Gifted with a passion for writing at a young age, Michaela has used this gift to minister to the Church by writing and teaching Bible study curricula for children, small groups, and women. Her involvement in multiple church ministries has blessed her with a unique perspective on discipleship and spiritual disciplines. She has a strong desire to help others experience deeper growth in their walk with Jesus by transparently sharing her own spiritual journey. She considers herself a "recovering perfectionist" because she is learning that if God's power works best in weakness, then she doesn't want to be perfect at all. Born in the beautiful Pacific Northwest, Michaela enjoys nothing more than spending time with her husband and daughter.

Learn more about her ministry at deeper-growth.com and follow her on social media:

***Facebook** @deeper.growth.mlc*
***Instagram** @deepergrowth.*

CPSIA information can be obtained
at www.ICGtesting.com
Printed in the USA
LVHW101947271122
734084LV00042B/298